A TREE A DAY

A Tree A Day

Amy-Jane Beer

BATSFORD

First published in the United Kingdom in 2021 by
B T Batsford Ltd
43 Great Ormond Street
London WC1N 3HZ

ISBN: 9781849946520

A CIP catalogue record for this book is available from the British Library.

30 29 28 27 26 25 24 23 22 21
10 9 8 7 6 5 4 3 2 1

Reproduction by Rival Colour Ltd, UK
Printed and bound by Toppan Leefung, China

This book can be ordered direct from the publisher at the website: www.pavilionbooks.com, or try your local bookshop.

Page 1: Quince tree, a chromolithography from 1870.

Previous page: A lone tree overlooks the North Kent Downs at sunset.

Above: The Irish tree alphabet (see page 208) spells out the author's dedication: To the tree lives threatened by needless, thoughtless or unjust felling.

Right: The forest floor of the New Forest in Hampshire.

CONTENTS

INTRODUCTION

Right: Bluebells carpet the floor in beautiful beech woodland.

Below: Humans and trees have been hanging out together since our very beginnings.

What is a tree? While most people have little difficulty naming a tree when they see one, hard-and-fast definitions are hard to pin down: there are exceptions to almost any simple rule of tree-hood. Trees are not a biologically distinct group. Rather the tree form has been adopted by a wide range of plants from a huge variety of taxonomic groups, and in its broadest sense the term can be applied to flowering and non-flowering plants, to monocots and dicots, to tall plants and small ones, upright and sprawling ones, woody plants and those with other means of making a rigid trunk such as tree ferns, palms and bamboos. Most, but not all, trees are woody plants, with one or more stems, known as trunks, and many, but not all, have the potential to grow tall.

In writing this book I've sought to address a different question: not what is a tree, but what do trees mean? Where do they fit in collectively and individually, to the web of experience that encompasses all life on Earth – including humans? I've explored some of those uncountable interactions and transactions in the following pages, but ultimately the question is a personal one. What does a tree mean you?

EMANCIPATION OAK
USA

The Emancipation Oak still stands near the entrance to Hampton University Virginia.

It was under this huge southern live oak (*Quercus virginiana*) in the small satellite town of Hampton, Virginia, that local people gathered in 1863 to hear the first Southern reading of President Abraham Lincoln's Emancipation Proclamation, which declared:

'That on the first day of January in the year of our Lord, one thousand eight hundred and sixty-three, all persons held as slaves within any State ... shall be then, thenceforward, and forever free.'

The tree is also linked with Mary Smith Peake, a free black woman, who defied state law to teach enslaved and free black Americans, continuing even as Civil War broke out. The oak under which her lessons took place was the first teaching space of what ultimately became Hampton University, on whose campus the oak still stands today.

THE MAJOR OAK
England

Loss of branches is a natural process in the veteran life stages of ancient trees, but like many much-loved specimens the Major Oak is supported by props to maintain its iconic shape.

Perhaps the best known of dozens of ancient pedunculate or English oaks in Britain, this vast, hollow specimen growing near the Nottinghamshire village of Edwinstowe is thought to be 900–1,000 years old. Its great age and location in Sherwood Forest have led to a strong association with the legend of Robin Hood. Could the outlaw and his men have rested in or beneath these spreading branches? The possibility is enough to draw hundreds of thousands of visitors a year along the gentle walk from the nearby visitor centre to view the tree. The name Major Oak commemorates Major Hayman Rooke, who wrote a book about notable trees of the area in 1790. Before that it had been known as the Queen's Oak and the Cockpen tree.

SOUTHERNMOST TREE

Above: The southernmost trees on Earth, Isla Hornos, Tierra del Fuego.

Top right: Mole discovers the reason river-bankers don't visit the Wild Wood, illustrated by Paul Bransom.

Bottom right: Joseph Tubb's poem grew with the tree for a further 170 years.

The southernmost trees on Earth live on the tip of South America – Isla Hornos (Cape Horn Island) off Tierra del Fuego. On eastern parts of the island trees grow in short, dense evergreen forests, offering shelter to breeding colonies of Magellanic penguins. South of the forest are isolated clumps of trees, growing in the shelter of rocky outcrops where they have some protection from the vicious storms for which Cape Horn is famed. Of these, the furthest south is a Magellan's beech (*Nothofagus betuloides*). It was identified and mapped in January 2019 during an expedition led by ecologists Brian Buma and Andrés Holz. The tree measured not more than 90cm (35½in) tall, with a trunk 10cm (4in) in diameter. A non-destructive ring count suggested it was 41 years old at the time of discovery.

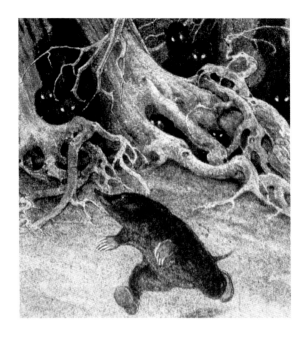

'*What lies over there?*' asked the Mole, waving a paw towards a wood that darkly framed the water-meadows on one side. 'That? O, that's just the Wild Wood,' said the Rat shortly. 'We don't go there very much, we river-bankers.'

The Wind in the Willows,
KENNETH GRAHAME (1908)

THE POEM TREE
Wittenham Clumps, England

*'As up the hill
   with labr'ing steps we tread
Where the twin Clumps
   their sheltering branches spread'*

These words formed part of a poem written and carved by local artist, Joseph Tubb, into the bark of a beech tree at Wittenham Clumps, Oxfordshire, between 1844 and 1845. The tree fell in 2012, but the spot is marked by a stone with a bronze plaque bearing a transcription of the poem, and a facsimile of the carving taken as a bark rubbing in 1965.

WASSAILING
England

Wassailing apple trees with hot cider in Devonshire on Twelfth Night. Illustrated London News (1861).

The tradition of wassailing in England marks the turn of the year and takes place in the days following the winter solstice. The celebrations begin at Yule or Christmas and culminate on Twelfth Night, when the slight lengthening of daylight hours begins to be perceptible. In some areas the wassailing tradition involves singing door-to-door in return for gifts of food and alcoholic beverages – a forerunner of both carolling and trick-or-treating. In cider-growing areas, however, the tradition focuses on orchards. Fruit trees are decorated (sometimes hung with pieces of toast), doused with cider and exhorted to produce a good crop in the coming year with singing and carousing.

OLIVE BRANCH
The Ancient Sisters, Lebanon

It is believed an olive branch from one of the Sisters, carried by a dove, signalled to Noah the approach of dry land during the great flood.

According to the Old Testament bible story, a dove flying out from Noah's Ark as it floated on the Great Flood, returned with a sprig of green from an olive tree, giving hope that the water must be receding and land not too far away.

Lebanese folklore suggests that the source of the branch is was a grove of trees growing in the small town of Bcheale. Known as the Ancient Sisters, the remaining sixteen trees are reputed to be 5000–6000 years old. This would set them among the world's oldest non-clonal trees, rivalling the bristlecone pines of California (see page 109).

The age of the trees has not been verified as their trunks are hollow. But they still produce fruit, which is made into highly marketable olive oil by a charity set up to care for the grove.

13

MONEY TREES
England

A wishing tree on the Ingleton Waterfalls Trail in the Yorkshire Dales, where visitors hammer a coin into the tree for luck.

In woodland around Britain there are fallen trees with hundreds of coins hammered into their decaying timber. While the tradition probably has Pagan origins and there are some reports of money trees in the 19th century, the practice appears to have undergone a strong revival in recent decades, in the north of England especially. A tree that fell in high winds at Bolton Abbey in the 1980s was dragged to the side of a popular footpath and soon began to accumulate coins. Now there are similar examples at beauty spots across the Yorkshire Dales and into Cumbria. It should go without saying that this kind of treatment would be highly damaging to living trees.

LAKE CHIVERO ROCK ART
Zimbabwe

One of several rock paintings, including one depicting the felling of a tree, at Lake Chivero Recreational Park near Harare, Zimbabwe.

It has sometimes been observed that plants are almost non-existent in prehistoric rock art. While pictures of animals abound, until around 5,000 years ago images of plants that the artists must have known and depended on are extremely rare. When they do begin to appear, they seem to be shown in a resource context. This finely rendered tree, which was painted at Bushman's Point on Lake Chivero, Zimbabwe, is a case in point. It dates from around 2,000 years ago, and judging by the small adjacent human figure wielding an axe, appears to show the tree as a commodity.

Left: The *Goshin* bonsai on display at the United States National Arboretum in Washington DC, to which it was donated by its creator John Yoshio Naka in 1984.

Opposite, top: Treebeard the Ent creaks to life in the 2002 movie *The Lord of the Rings: Two Towers.*

Opposite bottom: In this design, taken from the sarcophagus of the Mayan ruler Pakal, the long-reining monarch is shown lying at the foot of a cruciform World Tree.

GOSHIN
John Yoshio Naka (1948–1984)

A superlative example of the Japanese art of bonsai, *Goshin* (meaning 'protector of the spirit') is a group of 11 Foemina junipers (*Juniperus chinensis* var. 'Foemina') created by the Japanese-American horticulturalist John Yoshio Naka. The original composition, begun in 1948, comprised just two trees, to which Naka added over the years. By 1964 he had created a tiny forest of seven trees, one for each of his grandchildren. Four more grandchildren and four trees later, *Goshin* had reached its final composition. Of his painstakingly slow craft, Naka once said '... bonsai is not you working on the tree; you have to have the tree work on you.'

TREEBEARD

In the high-fantasy world of Middle Earth in J.R.R. Tolkein's epic *The Lord of the Rings*, Treebeard (also called Fangorn) is the oldest of the tree-like Ents, and hence the oldest living thing in the entire realm. He appears in *The Two Towers*, *The Return of the King* and also in the prequel *The Silmarillion*. Ents are gifted with a strange, deep wisdom; they are slow to react but immensely powerful when roused, and they play a key part in the battle against the dark wizard Saruman.

CEIBA TREE

In Mesoamerican mythology, the ceiba was a world tree or *axis mundi*, connecting the terrestrial world of humanity with the heavens and the terrifying underworld, *Xibalba* (meaning 'place of fright'). In other representations the trunk was sometimes depicted as a great caiman, standing on its tail. Real world ceibas are large, long-lived, spiny-trunked trees of Central and South America and the Caribbean. They include the kapok (*Ceiba pentandra*) whose seed fibres make great stuffing.

This reproduction from a fresco in the Roman city of Pompeii shows the nymph Daphne about to escape Apollo's clutches – note the sprouting laurel branch, the same colour as her mantle.

LAUREL OR DAPHNE
Laurus nobilis

This tree, whose glossy aromatic leaves are widely used in Mediterranean cooking and whose dense growth makes it a popular garden choice for hedging and topiary, was considered divine in the classical world. In Greek mythology, the goddess Daphne, daughter of Gaia, evaded the amorous advances of Apollo and left him with only a laurel tree to adore – he wore wreaths of the leaves ever after. The laurel continued to be a symbol of immortality to the Romans, and wreaths were worn by gods and emperors and bestowed on victors and champions as symbols of their accomplishments. The tradition is continued to this day in literal and symbolic form – for example, in portraiture, in the awarding of baccalaureate qualifications and laureateships.

COMMON DOGWOOD
Cornus sanguinea

Common dogwood is a familiar woodland understory tree in Europe and Asia, easily recognized by its oval leaves with widely spaced, curving veins. Another name, bloody dogwood, is a reference to its red winter stems, but is doubly apt given the suitability of its exceptionally hard wood and straight stems for making skewers, arrow-shafts and spears. This property was evidently well known to Neolithic people, and the mummified traveller known as Ötzi the Iceman, discovered in an alpine glacier in 1991, was carrying dogwood arrows in his quiver when he died over 5,000 years ago. As if to cement an already grim reputation, it is sometimes claimed that the cross on which Jesus Christ was crucified was also made of dogwood.

The glowing winter stems of dogwood mean it is a popular species in horticultural settings, where it provides spectacular seasonal colour.

COLLECTING MAPLE SAP
North America

Maple syrup is the concentrated sap from certain species of maple tree, usually the sugar maple (*Acer saccharum*) or black maple (*Acer nigrum*). Maples, like many deciduous trees of seasonal climates, store carbohydrates in their roots in the form of starch. In late winter, they mobilize this reserve, converting it into sugar and transporting it upwards ready to fuel the intense burst of spring growth.

Traditionally, this sap was tapped using a short spile – a metal or wooden tube with a pointed tip driven into the soft wood just under the bark, which contains thousands of tiny vessels that conduct sap up the trunk. Sap trickling from each spile was collected in a bucket and then boiled to reduce its volume about 40 times, resulting in the distinctively flavoured, super-sweet product. Modern systems tend to use plastic collecting bags or tubes that carry sap directly to a central evaporating unit.

Maple sap being tapped the traditional way. The trunks show the spile-scars of previous collections.

TREE OF TÉNÉRÉ
Niger

This poignant landmark in an otherwise empty landscape was once the world's most isolated tree.

Alone acacia growing in the Ténéré region of the Sahara Desert, some 350km (217 miles) from its nearest arboreal neighbour, was widely acknowledged as the world's most isolated tree until 1973. It was a remnant of the savanna landscape that existed before desertification of the region and a landmark so profound that its location remains marked on large-scale maps of the Sahara more than 45 years after it was somehow run over by a lorry. Its remains are held by the National Museum of Niger in Niamey, and a metal tree sculpture now stands in its place.

THE THERESIENSTADT (TEREZIN) TREE
Czech Republic

Artwork from the Theresienstadt ghetto (1942–1943). In 1944 the ghetto was 'beautified' by the Nazis for a Red Cross visit in Operation Embellishment. The ruse worked.

The Theresienstadt Ghetto was a concentration camp in the Czech town of Terezin. As part of a Nazi propaganda exercise, prisoners were allowed to practice religious and cultural activities and to educate their children. In 1943, in celebration of Tu B'Shvat, the Jewish 'New Year of the Trees', a teacher-detainee called Irma Lauscher planted a smuggled sycamore cutting, and encouraged the children to tend it. Of more than 15,000 children passing through Theresienstadt *en route* to Auschwitz, fewer than 200 survived the war. But thanks to their care, and that of their inspirational teacher, the tree lived on into the 21st century. Its preserved trunk stands in the grounds of the memorial Ghetto Museum and hundreds of descendants nurtured from its seeds now grow in commemorative locations around the world. Tu B'Shvat falls in January or February of the Gregorian calendar.

23

MORETON BAY FIG OR AUSTRALIAN BANYAN
Ficus macrophylla

A Moreton Bay fig growing in Kings Park in Perth, Western Australia, displays the buttress roots and multiple trunks typical of the species.

These potentially enormous trees begin life as epiphytes – germinating from seeds deposited in the branches of host trees and putting out shoots that descend to the ground to root as well as growing up and out, thickening so that they can support themselves when the host tree dies from strangulation. Mature specimens are distinguished by massive buttress roots, and in some forms by curtains of aerial roots that drop from branches to the ground. The species is native to eastern Australia but has been introduced widely to tropical and warm temperate parts of the world.

THE LONE CYPRESS
USA

The Lone Cypress is reputed to be the most photographed tree in North America, and has been trademarked by the local community.

This iconic tree growing on a rocky outcrop above Pebble Beach, on the Monterey Peninsula near Carmel in California, is a Monterey cypress (*Hesperocyparis macrocarpa*, previously known as *Cupressus macrocarpa*). Thought to have been fairly widespread in prehistoric times, the species' native range is now restricted to two small populations at Pebble Beach and nearby Lobos Point, though it has been introduced elsewhere, notably in New Zealand.

KIIDK'YAAS
(THE GOLDEN SPRUCE)
Canada

A highly unusual golden-needled example of Sitka spruce (*Picea sitchensis* 'Aurea') growing on the largest of the Haida Gwaii islands off the coast of British Columbia, and thought to be over 300 years old, was considered sacred to the First Nation Haida people. However, the tree became more famous for the tragedy of its felling in a delusional act of protest by a local logger called Grant Hadwin. By his own account, on 20th January 1997, Hadwin swam the freezing river with a specially purchased chainsaw and cut the tree in such a way that it fell as soon as the wind picked up two days later. Hadwin claimed to be motivated by hatred of 'university-trained professors and their extremist supporters'. In the run-up to his trial, public outrage was so great that he claimed to fear for his life and refused to take public transport. Instead he set off to court by kayak, and disappeared. His wrecked boat was found months later but Hadwin was never seen again. The mystery of his ultimate fate – drowned, murdered or escaped – has never been solved.

In the mythology of the Haida people, this golden spruce was once a boy who was transfigured as a supernatural punishment for dishonouring nature.

COCO DE MER OR SEA COCONUT
Lodoicea maldivica

Coco de mer
on the beach of
Anse Boudin,
Seychelles.

The *coco de mer* was first described from huge seeds washed up on beaches of the Maldives, where they were sometimes attributed with supernatural undersea origins. The seeds are the largest of any known plant, occasionally weighing more than 17kg (37½lb), and they come from the heaviest known wild fruit – a double (bilobed) coconut weighing up to 42kg (92½lb). These extraordinary fruits take six or seven years to mature, and a further two years to germinate.

The popular idea that the tree relied on a long-haul dispersal strategy in which the nuts travelled vast distances by sea belies that fact that the natural distribution of the species is restricted to a handful of islands in the Seychelles. In truth, viable nuts are much too dense to be able to float, and those occasionally found drifting thousands of miles away are rotten.

'I THINK ...'
DARWIN'S PHYLOGENETIC TREE OF LIFE

The tree-like diagrams used to show relationships between organisms or species descended from a shared common ancestor are called cladograms. An early version sketched by Charles Darwin in a notebook and never published in his lifetime has become an icon of evolutionary thinking. The original notebook is one of two that went missing from Cambridge University Library in 2000, and which are now presumed to have been stolen.

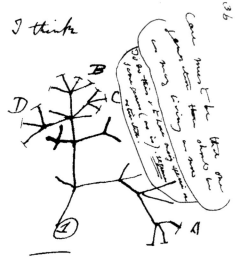

Charles Darwin's first diagram of an evolutionary tree, a sketch from his First notebook on transmutation of species (1837).

TREE SCULPTURE
Maelstrom, Roxy Paine (2009)

Maelstrom is seen here during its six-month run on the roof of the Metropolitan Museu m of Art in Manhattan in 2009.

American artist Roxy Paine is perhaps best known for the huge tree-like sculptures he calls 'dendroids'. They are constructed to mathematical rules similar to those that govern real tree forms. *Maelstrom* is intended to represent the swirling, crackling energy of a storm and its impact on a forest, and also, says Paine, the idea of a 'mental storm, or what I envision happens during an epileptic seizure'.

CHIPKO ANDOLAN
India

Chipko Andolan is an environmental movement which was formed in the 1970s in the sub-Himalayan state of Uttarakhand in India by villagers protesting the increasingly rapacious exploitation of forests by commercial logging of ash trees. The movement allied itself closely with the sacrifice of Amrita Devi and 363 other Bishnoi Hindus some 240 years previously (see page 265). While the Chipko leaders were men, women were key to its impact and to the effectiveness of its non-violent direct action. Chipko founder Sunderlal Bahuguna inspired a generation of activists with his assertion that 'Ecology is the permanent economy.'

Left: The Chipko movement helped to bring the term 'tree hugger' into mainstream usage.

Top right: Blue tit resting on a dogwood branch in winter.

Bottom right: An oak seedling after one summer's growth.

WINTER FIRE

Cultivars of common dogwood (*Cornus sanguinea*) are grown for the spectacular colour of their bare twigs in winter, but also for practical purposes. The fruits of dogwood, while not generally eaten by people, are hugely popular with birds and are thus often grown close to cherry and plum orchards in order to distract from the main crop.

'*A human being is bred with a unique set of potentials that yearn to be fulfilled as surely as the acorn yearns to become the oak within it.*'

ARISTOTLE, GREEK POLYMATH AND PHILOSOPHER (384–322 BCE)

MALHAM ASH
England

A solitary ash dominates the much-filmed and photographed landscape above Malham Cove in North Yorkshire.

A solitary ash (*Fraxinus excelsior*) growing on the limestone plateau of Malham Cove in the Yorkshire Dales is one of the most photographed trees in Britain – as well as one of the hardiest. The strange rock formations, known as limestone pavement, are made up of irregularly shaped blocks (clints) and deep weathered fissures (grykes). The plateau is fiercely exposed, but the grykes provide sheltered microcosms in which a wonderful diversity of plants can thrive, and despite first impressions, there is usually plenty of water which the tree accesses via roots penetrating deep into ever-smaller cracks and crevices in the rock.

Tree Horsetail
Calamites spp.

The distinctively whorled leaves of ancient horsetails show clearly in fossils more than 300 million years old from Saxony in Germany.

In modern times, horsetails such as *Equisetum* spp. are familiar plants of damp places, rarely growing more than 1m (3¼ft) high. But over 300 million years ago, giant horsetails, such as *Calamites* spp., were among the dominant tall vegetation. Some grew as tall as 50m (164ft), supported on woody stems, which were hollow and noded rather like those of bamboo, but with pronounced vertical ribbing. The filamentous leaves were borne on whorls, in a similar way to modern horsetails.

THE DARK HEDGES
Northern Ireland

An avenue of around 150 beeches planted along the approach to Gracehill House in County Antrim, Northern Ireland, in the late 18th century forms a strikingly atmospheric tunnel. The location appeared as the Kings Road in the blockbuster HBO TV series *Game of Thrones*, adding greatly to its tourist appeal. When two of the huge trees were felled by the high winds of Storm Gertrude in January 2016, their timber was carved into ten elaborately decorative doors, based on scenes from Season Six of the show. The doors are now fitted in pubs and bars close to other *Game of Thrones* filming locations.

The stately limbs and glowering shade of ancient beeches of Ulster's Dark Hedges create an irresistible cinematic atmosphere.

Euphorbiaceae
(Acalypheae)

Hevea brasiliensis Müll. Arg.

PARÁ RUBBER TREE
Hevea brasiliensis

The rubber tree, as illustrated in the 19th-century herbal *Köhler's Medicinal Plants* by Hermann Adolph Köhler.

One of the largest members of the spurge family (Euphorbiaceae), the rubber tree grows over 40m (130ft) tall in its natural state. It is native to the Amazon rainforest, where its latex was harvested by indigenous people. However, rubber trees became botanical gold following the refinement of the vulcanization process by Henry Goodyear, resulting in a more elastic and less perishable product. In 1876, the explorer Henry Wickham stole and smuggled a large consignment of rubber seeds out of Brazil to Kew Gardens in England, and the plants that germinated were used to start vast plantations in the British and Dutch colonies of India, Ceylon (Sri Lanka), Malaya (Malaysia), the East Indies (Indonesia) and Singapore.

STRANGLERS OF ANGKOR
Cambodia

In the ancient ruins of Ta Prohm temple close to Angkor Wat, vast trees appear to be part of the architecture.

The vast 12th-century temple city of Angkor Wat in Siem Reap, Cambodia, was built to last – but centuries of neglect following the decline of the Khmer Empire gave nature an opportunity to take advantage in emphatic style. In parts of the complex, stonework has been variously shattered, prized apart and almost completely engulfed by the roots and shoots of banyans (*Ficus* spp.), kapok or silk cottons (*Ceiba pentandra*) and thitpok trees (*Tetrameles nudiflora*). That the trees have been able reach such sizes rooted in masonry seems extraordinary – but the sandstone from which the temples are constructed is unusually porous, permitting the percolation of sufficient moisture to supply the roots. While some parts of the temple complex are beyond restoration, further tree growth is now strictly controlled by nimble-footed gardeners, who shun ropes and scaffolding that would damage the stonework or obscure it from view. They work instead with secateurs, long ladders and nerves of steel.

LAM TSUEN WISHING TREE
Hong Kong, China

The Lam Tsuen wishing trees hung with replica oranges and wish tags during the celebrations of the Lunar New Year.

The stately Chinese banyan trees (*Ficus microcarpa*) in the grounds of Tin Hau Temple in Fong Ma Po, Hong Kong, are the traditional focus of lunar New Year celebrations. Local people would write wishes on red joss paper scrolls tied to oranges, which were thrown into the branches. If the string caught, the wish was to be granted. The paper and oranges made a striking display, but as the trees aged, the weight of fruit became too much, and in 2005 an elderly man and a child were injured when a branch fell. As a consequence, the oranges used now are made from plastic and they are thrown, not into the banyans, but into replica trees.

MENARA
Borneo

Yellow merantis are part of the emergent layer of the Bornean rainforest – their crowns towering over the canopy formed by less lofty species.

The Danum Valley, in the Malaysian state of Sabah in Borneo, is home to the world's tallest flowering plant, a yellow meranti tree (*Shorea faguetiana*). Nicknamed Menara, meaning 'tower' in Malay, the tree was discovered in 2014 and LiDAR scanned (see page 306) by a team from Oxford University and University College London. Further terrestrial laser scanning, manual measurements of the base and a drone survey carried out in 2018 provided tantalizing details of its gigantic stature and estimated its mass at 81.5 metric tonnes. Then, in January 2019, conservationist and tree climber Unding Jami scaled the tree and dropped a tape from its very top, confirming its height at 100.8m (331ft), 30cm (12in) taller than the previous angiosperm record-holder, a mountain ash known as Centurion (see page 199).

SUMMONING HELP

The caterpillar of the pine hawkmoth (*Sphinx pinastri*) is targeted by parasitoid ichneumon wasps, which help ensure the trees are not over exploited.

Studies of several species of tree including pines and elms have revealed some astounding alliances with certain species of parasitic wasps, involving a kind of interspecies chemical communication. When one of these trees is attacked by caterpillars, a particular aromatic compound is released, not just from the damaged leaves, but by every leaf on the tree. This compound is recognized by the female parasitic wasps, which fly in and inject their eggs inside the bodies of the caterpillars using a needle-like ovipositor. The wasp grub quickly kills the caterpillar and the tree gains respite from the caterpillar attack. Most impressively, the distress signal that recruits the wasps is only released in response to caterpillar saliva – other kinds of damage, such as snipping of leaves with scissors, or browsing by deer – does not trigger the same cry for help.

BORTH SUBMERGED FOREST
Wales

Winter storms and low tides occasionally combine to expose the preserved remains of forests that grew on the coast of Ceredigion in the Bronze Age.

On the coast of Ceredigion in West Wales between Borth and Ynyslas, the fossilized remains of an ancient forest can be seen during very low tides. The rising sea levels that drowned this forest thousands of years ago are recalled in the rich folklore of the area, especially the tale of Cantre'r Gwaelod, a kingdom lost under the sea. The preserved stumps are those of pine, oak, alder and birch, which, according to carbon-dating studies, died between 4,500 and 6,000 years ago.

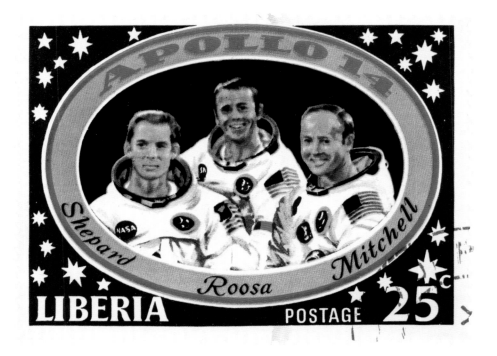

MOON TREES

Above: Members of the Apollo 14 mission touched down on the moon on 5th February 1971.

Top right: An elegant avenue of hornbeams in Dortmund, Germany.

Bottom right: The distinctively marked bark of downy birch, scored with horizontal lenticels.

During the Apollo 14 space mission in February 1971, while Alan Shepard and Edgar Mitchell bounced and hit golf balls on the lunar surface, their colleague and pilot of the command module, Stuart Roosa, remained in orbit. He carried with him a packet of 500 seeds given to him by the US Forest Service. The journey seems not to have done them any harm. Back on Earth, 420 of the well-travelled seeds germinated successfully, and from 1973 onwards the Moon Trees they grew into – a mixture of sycamore, sweetgum, redwood, loblolly pine and Douglas fir – were gifted by Roosa and his daughter Rosemary around the world. The most recent, a loblolly pine (*Pinus taeda*), was replanted at NASA's Johnson Space Centre in Houston, Texas in 2016.

EUROPEAN HORNBEAM
Carpinus betulus

The supremely elegant hornbeam has leaves superficially similar to those of beech but finely toothed, and they retain slight alternating pleats all summer. The papery, green-veined fruits of hornbeam are known as samaras. They hang in bunches and when ripe they attract large flocks of birds, including finches and tits. The hornbeam is prized for the strength of its timber and is often coppiced to encourage it to produce more stems.

DOWNY BIRCH
Betula pubescens

A close relative of silver birch, the downy birch can be identified by the fuzz of soft hairs on small stems and leaf stalks, and the abundance of horizontal scars (lenticels) on its bark, which is usually greyish-brown rather than white, and lacks the papery 'peelability' of silver birch. However, the two species hybridize readily, making identification potentially tricky. Downy birch is the most northerly growing broadleaved tree in the world, occurring well into the Arctic.

THE NO PARKING TREE
Sorbus admonitor

As of 2020, with its trunk hollow and rotting, the original No Parking tree appears to be nearing the end of its life.

This rare hybrid whitebeam is found only in the mixed woodlands around Watersmeet in North Devon. It was first noticed in 1930, growing in a lay-by with a 'No Parking' sign nailed to its trunk. It drew attention because, while it was clearly a whitebeam, its leaves were curiously lobed. It took 21st-century molecular analysis to finally prove the distinctive tree was a species in its own right in 2009, by which time just over 100 further specimens had been located in the area.

TREE
Tania Kovats (2009)

Ceiling artwork at the Natural History Museum, London, made from a 17m (56ft) montage of slices from a 200-year-old oak tree and aptly named *Tree*.

This spectacular installation was commissioned to mark the 200th birthday of Charles Darwin, and the 150th anniversary of the publication of his most famous work, *On the Origin of Species*. The concept was inspired by Darwin's tree of life (see page 28), but the tree is a real one – a 200-year-old oak that grew on the Longleat Estate in Wiltshire. The tree was replaced by 200 new saplings, which will, in time, form a commemorative grove, and the crater created when the roots were excavated was turned into a wildlife pond. Thin slices of the trunk and the major branches were used to create this striking montage on the ceiling of the Cadogan Gallery at the Natural History Museum in London. Further slices were distributed to museums in countries visited by Darwin on his historic expedition aboard the *HMS Beagle*.

RED MANGROVE
Rhizophora mangle

The roots of red mangrove knit the edges of many Caribbean islands, providing both shelter and erosion control.

The red mangrove is a tropical species adapted to grow in tidal habitats where it tolerates waterlogged, oxygen-depleted conditions and concentrations of salt that would be fatal to most other flowering plants. Native to coasts on both sides of the Atlantic, the red mangrove creates dense stands in relatively sheltered shallow coastal waters. Its aerial roots boost oxygen uptake, but ingeniously also serve as props to support the branches, allowing the tree to spread very wide over the high-water mark.

THE ANTHROPOCENE TREE OR THE LONELIEST TREE
Campbell Island

The sole survivor of an ill-advised forestry scheme, this lonely Sitka spruce now boasts sobering new significance for its role in defining the Anthropocene epoch.

A single shrubby Sitka spruce (*Picea sitchensis*), growing on the bleak outpost of Campbell Island (*Motu Ihupuku* in Maori) some 600km (373 miles) south of New Zealand, is the world's most remote living tree. It is not native – the subantarctic climate of the island is singularly unsuited to forestation – but the sole survivor of a plantation commissioned by Uchter Knox, Earl of Ranfurly and governor of New Zealand, in the early 1900s. Perhaps a more lasting claim to fame for the tree is as a marker for the start of the geological epoch known as the Anthropocene. Analysis of its wood showed a spike in radioactive carbon in the growth ring laid down in 1965 – an echo of the above-ground nuclear tests carried out in the Pacific Ocean during the 1950s and '60s. Scientists regard this as an appropriate marker for the moment in time when human activity became the dominant influence on the planet.

HACHI NO KI
Japan

In a traditional woodblock print by Toshikata Mizuno, the impoverished Sano Tsuneyo lights a fire with the branches of his prized bonsai trees.

The Japanese art of *hachi no ki*, which translates as 'the potted tree', is a precursor of bonsai, in which trees are grown in small containers that restrict their growth. In *hachi no ki* the containers are bowls, with more root space than is available to true, tray-grown bonsai. The term is also the title of a 14th-century Noh play about a poor and aging samurai, Tsuneyo Genzayemon, who destroys his coveted trees – a plum, a pine and a cherry – and uses them as firewood when he is visited by needy monk. It later transpires that the monk is Hōjō Tokiyori, regent to the shogunate, travelling in disguise, and Tsuneyo is rewarded for his selflessness.

BOG OAK

The dark hue of this vintage bog-oak trinket box is the result of staining by tannin rich water.

Bog oak, also known as bog wood, black wood, morta or abonos, is wood that has been preserved by long immersion in a peat bog, where anaerobic and acidic conditions prevent normal decay. The water in the bogs is rich in tannins, which darken and harden the wood over hundreds or thousands of years. Despite the common name, bog oak comes from a variety of tree species, though oak, yew and pine are among the most commonly recovered. Bog oak fetches a high price for carving and furniture making.

NELLIE'S TREE
England

Around a century ago, a young miner called Vic Stead from Garforth, West Yorkshire, was in the habit of taking regular walks to visit his sweetheart, Nellie, in the nearby village of Aberford. It occurred to him to create a living tribute to her by grafting three beech saplings to form the letter 'N'. The couple were married and Nellie's Tree grew into a local landmark.

CHERRY PLUM
Prunus cerasifera

The ancestor of the domesticated plum, the cherry plum grows wild and in a variety of cultivated forms across western Eurasia. It is valued as an ornamental tree or shrub thanks to its prolific blossom, which is often the first to appear in late winter. The early supply of nectar makes it a popular choice for wildlife gardens, and it will often be humming with insect life on milder days in February. The fruits are variable in colour and sweetness.

THE THREE TREES
Rembrandt (1643)

There is more to this highly detailed etching by the Dutch master than immediately meets the eye. Three trees dominate the scene, but look more closely and you will see that there are carters passing on the road behind the trees to the right, herds of cows are loitering in the middle distance, and a man is fishing on the left while his female companion could not appear more bored. An artist perched sketching on the slope below the trees is seen as a small silhouette. But have any of these characters noticed the romantic assignation in the heavy shade of the bushes in the foreground?

'The greatest achievement was at first and for a time a dream. The oak sleeps in the acorn, the bird waits in the egg, and in the highest vision of the soul a waking angel stirs. Dreams are the seedlings of realities.'

JAMES ALLEN, BRITISH PHILOSOPHER AND SELF-HELP PIONEER (1864–1912)

RAKAU MOMORI
New Zealand

Above: High tech scanning is now needed to preserve the mysterious Chatham Island dendroglyphs.

Left: *Talking to a Tree* (uncredited).

The Chatham Islands (Rēkohu) lie 840km (522 miles) east of New Zealand and support a small permanent population of around 600 people. In wooded areas, images known as *rakau momori* carved mainly on the trunks of karaka trees (*Corynocarpus laevigatus*) feature human forms and naturalistic motifs. The name translates approximately as 'memories in wood', and it is speculated that the images may have been created as memorials or ancestor tributes, but no one living knows exactly what they meant to the Moriori islanders who carved them. The area where most of the *rakau momori* exist is protected as the J.M. Barker (Hāpūpū) National Historic Reserve, but because the lives of trees are finite, many carvings have already been lost. In a bid to preserve their mystery, many of those that remain have been scanned using 3D laser technology, which will allow future generations to ponder their meaning for centuries to come.

MEIRIONNYDD OAKWOODS
The Welsh Rainforests

Welsh rainforest, where sessile oak, known in Wales as Welsh oak, provides habitat for hundreds of species.

Saved from clearance and overgrazing largely by virtue of steep gradients, a cluster of woodlands in the historic north Welsh county of Meirionnydd (now part of Gwynedd) give a tantalizing insight into the verdant landscape this once was. The area receives over 1m (3¼ft) of rain a year and water is everywhere, cascading in steep streams, dripping from the canopy, misting the air, seeping through moss and moistening the crevices of tree bark. The woods are dominated by sessile oak (*Quercus petraea*) which, as its scientific name suggests (*petraea* comes from Greek, meaning 'dwelling in rocky places'), is well-suited to rocky habitats, although almost no surface is unvegetated. The woodlands are famed for their diversity of mosses, liverworts, lichens and ferns, which lend a primordial, Tolkienesque vibe.

LORD OF THE FOREST
Denys Watkins-Pitchford, 'BB' (1975)

BB studied at the Royal College of Art and always illustrated his own books.

*L*ord of the Forest, by the English naturalist, countryman and prolific author Denys Watkins-Pitchford, writing under the pseudonym 'BB', is the story of a single oak, which grows from an acorn planted by a young swineherd in the year 1272. The story weaves together the life of the tree with those of the people and the wildlife that come and go alongside it, though a vast swathe of English history until September 1944. Like all BB's books, *Lord of the Forest* begins with the following instruction:

'The wonder of the world
The beauty and the power,
The shapes of things,
Their colours, lights and shades,
These I saw.
Look ye also while life lasts.'

TAPION PÖTYA (TAPIO'S TABLE)
Finland

An 1894 illustration from the epic Finnish poem the *Kalevala*. Around 75 per cent of Finland's land area is covered in forest, making it ideal for mythical forest-dwellers.

In the Finnish creation myth, first written down in the form of an epic poem, the *Kalevala*, Tapio is a forest deity akin to a Green Man (see page 85), cloaked in moss, with a fur hat and a beard of shaggy lichen. He is king of the bears, and of the forest realm of Tapiola. A mortal planning to hunt or bring livestock to forage in his forest was well-advised to present offerings at a ritual site known as *Tapion pötya* or 'Tapio's table'. Tapio's wife was the goddess Mielikki, healer and guardian of smaller forest animals.

THE HALL OF MOSSES
USA

The temperate rainforests of the Olympic National Park in Washington State receive around 1.2m (4ft) of rain in a year. Rich soils and an abundance of water discourage the trees (mostly conifers such as Sitka spruce, Douglas fir and western red cedar) from putting down deep or extensive roots, and so large specimens fall relatively easily. The result is an enormous matrix of standing and dead wood, each with its own ecosystem of epiphytes and other life. Mosses are especially abundant, cloaking every available surface in a shaggy pelt of vivid green.

The Hoh Rainforest is the wettest place in the contiguous Unites States.

ANNE FRANKBOOM (ANNE FRANK TREE)
The Netherlands

'Nearly every morning I go to the attic to blow the stuffy air out of my lungs, from my favourite spot on the floor I look up at the blue sky and the bare chestnut tree, on whose branches little raindrops shine, appearing like silver, ... As long as this exists, I thought, and I may live to see it, this sunshine, the cloudless skies, while this lasts I cannot be unhappy.'

FROM *The Diary of a Young Girl*, ANNE FRANK

Above: Anne Frank writing in her family's former home before they were forced into hiding in 1942.

Right: The tall chestnut tree in central Amsterdam that brought comfort to Anne Frank no longer stands, but saplings from its seeds now grow in her memory around the world.

The diary of Anne Frank, a young German-Dutch Jewish girl written during the Second World War became a global phenomenon when it was published posthumously in 1947. This extract from 23rd February 1944 describes a horse-chestnut Anne could see from the hidden annexe in her father's office building on Prinsengracht canal in Amsterdam. Anne hid in the annexe for two years with her family and four other people during the Nazi occupation. She died in Belsen concentration camp in February or March 1945, a few weeks before the camp was liberated. The street tree she loved became synonymous with her legacy, but was blown down in a storm on 23rd August 2010.

THE MINISTERS AND THEIR CRONIES OFF TO BOTANY BAY, AND THE DORCHESTER MEN RETURNING.

TOLPUDDLE MARTYR'S TREE
England

A gleeful political cartoon from 1836 shows the pardonned Martyrs returning home, while 'ministers and their cronies' are dispatched to serve punishment.

Large trees have long served as meeting places for rural folk, but the assembly of six farm labourers under a sycamore in the Dorset village of Tolpuddle in 1833 was to have more significant consequences than most. The six men were angry at the way in which their wages were steadily declining, and the organization they formed, the Friendly Society of Agricultural Labourers, was an early form of trades union. Its members refused to work for less than 10 shillings a week. While this in itself was not a crime, it enraged local landowners, and on the 24th of February 1834 the society's six founders were arrested. They were later prosecuted and convicted under an obscure piece of legislation that forbade the swearing of secret oaths. The sentence was transportation and seven years penal labour in Australia. Public outcry and one of the first political marches in the UK saw the Martyrs pardoned in 1836. They returned home as popular heroes, but five of the six later emigrated to Ontario, Canada.

CORK FOREST
Spain

Cork stripped from the lower trunk of cork oaks regrows over a period of around 10 years.

Cork is the spongy, protective cambium tissue of the evergreen cork oak, *Quercus suber*, which is native to the Mediterranean region. Cork is a renewable resource, which can be harvested repeatedly and sustainability from living trees. One harvest from a good tree will yield enough material for around 4000 wine corks. While they can't be described as natural, well-managed forests such as this one in southern Spain are among the most precious and potentially biodiverse habitats in the world. They are also highly endangered, as a result of the replacement of cork products with alternatives made from synthetic materials, and in particular the increasing use of plastic stoppers and metal screw caps on wine bottles. Declining demand threatens to make cork production uneconomic – something to consider with your next purchase of wine.

KODAMA TREES
Japan

A *shimenawa* rope
with paper *shide*
around a tree at
Atsuta Shinto
Shrine in
Nagoya, Japan.

In Japanese folklore, *kodama* trees are those inhabited by forest spirits, also called *kodama*. It is said that the voices of *kodama* can be heard as echoes in mountain landscapes. Felling such a tree will bring a curse or other misfortune, and so they are often marked with shrines or lengths of thick *shimenawa* rope to help prevent an unlucky mistake.

CLOUD FOREST

At certain altitudes in tropical landscapes, the air cools to a point where the water vapour it carries begins to condense – forming clouds or fog. The cool, saturated, low-light conditions of cloud forests make for slower growth, and acidic conditions on the ground lead to the build-up of peaty soils. The trees that grow in such places tend to be smaller than those at lower altitudes, and are often cloaked in a thick pelt of mosses, ferns and other epiphytes. Cloud forests are extraordinarily wet – even when is it not raining, water condensing on foliage creates a type of internal precipitation known as fog drip.

The mostly virgin cloud forest around Monteverde in Costa Rica was protected in 1972 and became one of the world's first ecotourism destinations.

KITAYAMA DAISUGI
Japan

This spectacular *daisugi* cedar grows in the peaceful grounds of Sorenji Buddist Temple in Kitayama.

The Japanese silviculture practice of *daisugi* (meaning 'platform tree') is a form of pollarding developed over half a millennium ago as a sustainable means of growing and harvesting timber. Stems cut from a mature cedar regrow, perfectly straight, flexible and exceptionally strong, and are thus ideal for use in many areas of construction in a region prone to both typhoons and earthquakes. The stems, known as *taruki* are particularly associated with a style of roofing seen in traditional tea houses. Kyoto is the home of *daisugi* – the technique began there as a way of conserving existing forests. It is also home to this, the most famous example, which grows in the Kitayama district of the city.

OLIVE TREES
Vincent van Gogh (1889)

Vincent van Gogh returned time and again to the olive groves around Saint-Rémy-de-Provence. He painted this view in June 1889, the same month he produced *The Starry Night*.

Perhaps the most iconic tree in Mediterranean culture, the European olive has been cultivated for at least 7,000 years. Its main use, in the production of oil for culinary, ceremonial and conditioning purposes, is so ancient and ubiquitous that the word 'oil' is derived from its Greek name, *olea*. It is also a valued timber tree and its branches have been used as a symbol of victory and peace for millennia.

In this, one of many Van Gogh paintings of olive trees, conservators recently discovered the remains of grasshopper embedded in the thick paint. Presumably the insect hopped on to the canvas as Van Gogh worked.

SACRED FIG OR PEEPAL TREE
Ficus religiosa

An anonymous
18th-century
Tibetan Buddhist
painting depicts
Amitabha, The
Buddha of eternal
life, in his paradise,
Sukhavati, also
known as the
Western Pure Land.

This potentially long-lived species has held special significance in
Hinduism, Jainism and Buddhism for millennia (see also pages 303
and 341). It is regarded as a form of world tree and home of the gods, and is
referred to in the sacred Hindu text, the *Bhagavad Gita*, where Lord Krishna
declares 'Of all the trees, I am the peepal tree.' The Sadhus of Hinduism
and Jainism traditionally practice ascetic meditation under the branches
of a sacred fig, either sitting or pacing around it, and it was at the end of
such a meditation that Siddhartha Gautama was 'awakened' to become the
Buddha. In life the tree is recognized by its heart-shaped leaves with a long
narrow 'drip tip'.

TREE OGHAM
Wales and Ireland

Tree ogham symbols carved into short sections of branches from the appropriate species are used as divining tools in neopaganism.

Ogham is an ancient form of writing known mainly from inscriptions (usually names) on stone monuments dating from the early medieval period, mainly in Ireland and Wales. The origins of the alphabet run back at least to the 4th century CE, perhaps earlier, and it remained in use until the 10th century. The writing comprises an alphabet (the *Beith-Luis-Nin*) of 20 characters or *feda*, whose names are based on those of native tree species, from *beith* (birch) to *Iodhadh* (yew).

Oak Tree, Centre of England, Lillington, Nr. Leamington.

THE MIDLAND OAK
England

The former Midland Oak, as it appeared in 1909.

The Midland Oak, in Leamington Spa, Warwickshire, stands at what was long reputed to be the geographic centre of England. The current tree is a replacement, said to be a direct descendant of the original. In fact, the location of the centre of England is hotly disputed – with other claims (each citing different means of calculation) from the villages of Meriden near Coventry, Morton in Derbyshire and Lindley Hall Farm in Leicestershire.

VIRGINIAN WITCH HAZEL
Hamamelis virginiana

The flowering of witch hazel in the coldest part of the year contributes to its supernatural reputation and its American nickname of 'winterbloom'.

One of five species of witch hazel, this one is native to North America. Witch hazel is a small, shrubby woodland tree, notable for flowering in autumn and winter, when the branches are otherwise bare. The somewhat straggly-looking blooms are yellow to red, highly scented and feature long, narrow petals. Decoctions made by boiling shoots and stems were widely used in Native American medicine and the practice was quickly adopted by settlers. The astringent, soothing properties of witch hazel water and ointments are widely used in the treatment of skin rashes, haemorrhoids and after childbirth. Despite this, the origin of the common name is nothing to do with witches, but from the Old English *wice*, meaning 'flexible'.

LOTE TREE OR SIDR

Celtis australis is variously known as the European nettle tree, Mediterranean hackberry, lote tree, or honeyberry. Botanical illustration by Edouard Maubert.

In Islam, the Lote tree or Sidr is an iteration of the Tree of Life. It appears in the Qur'an, both on Earth and in paradise, and it marks the limit of the seventh and highest heaven – the very last living thing in all creation. As an earthly tree it is usually associated with a species of *Ziziphus* – either *Z. lotus* or *Z. spina-christi*, both of which also have extensive mythologies in other religions and cultures (see page 301 and page 88), or with the Mediterranean hackberry, *Celtis australis*.

SAKURA
Jo Stephen (2018)

The title *Sakura* references the Japanese love of cherry blossom (see also page 72).

Jo Stephen is a photographic artist who uses creative processing techniques to reveal some of the magic felt in moments of connection with nature. Of *Sakura* she says, 'Like most of my work this image was taken not in Japan, but in the immediate landscape around my village home in North Dorset. The ethos behind my practise is developing my connection and kinship to the nature around me and keeping my carbon footprint as low as possible. Greeting the first delicate and resilient blossom of spring is always an eagerly anticipated moment, signalling longer days and the return of the light.'

HANAMI
Japan

The ephemeral beauty of blossom time brings huge crowds to tree-lined avenues and parks in Tokyo and other Japanese cities.

*H*anami or blossom viewing is a centuries-old springtime tradition across Japan, where groves of *sakura* or cherry trees put on a short-lived but sublimely beautiful display. The earliest blossoms appear in the southernmost prefecture of Okinawa in February, and celebrations move gradually north with the season. Viewings take place by day and at night. Feasts and picnics are held in parks and coloured lanterns twinkle among the blossoms.

PUSSY WILLOW
Salix caprea

The pollen-covered male catkins of pussy willow are a conspicuous sign of early spring.

This typically small, shrubby tree, also known as goat willow or great sallow, shares a liking for damp and waterside places with other willows. It stands out in late winter when male trees develop catkins covered with the softest of grey fur – like the paws of tiny kittens or baby rabbits. As these 'pussy-kins' open, they put out yellow stamens and cast pollen into the air to fertilize the longer, greener catkins of female trees. Both male and female trees produce catkins well before leaves, allowing free passage of pollen. The flowering branches are often cut and brought indoors, and can be dried and displayed for years.

MYTHAGO WOOD
Robert Holdstock (1984)

'The oakwoods were melded together into a grey-green blur'. (*Mythago Wood*)

In the critically-acclaimed cycle of fantasy novels by Robert Holdstock, an ancient English woodland contains a parallel universe inhabited by mythic characters and creatures generated from the imaginations of people living nearby, with powerful elements of shamanism, and English and Celtic folklore. Space and time are vastly different within the wood, and those drawn inside, including estranged brothers and an obsessive scientist determined to unravel the mysteries of the place, experience terrifying ordeals. At the centre of the wood lies Lavondyss, its oldest, darkest and most magical realm. In one sequence, the heroine of the second book, Tallis, endures many gruelling lifetimes as tree and wood before being restored to her young life outside.

COFFEE
Coffea arabica

Coffee 'beans' are in fact the seeds of small, fleshy cherry-like fruits known as drupes.

The Arabian or mountain coffee tree was the first species of *Coffea* to be cultivated for its beans, as long ago as the 12th century. Arab scholars noted its effect on their powers of concentration and ability to work for long hours.

The coffee tree is distinguished by glossy dark green leaves and sprays of white flowers, which when seen up close reveal its affiliation to the bedstraw family. It's now grown extensively in Central and South America, Central and East Africa, the Indian subcontinent and Southeast Asia and Indonesia and coffee beans are the second biggest export of developing nations worldwide.

THE FREETOWN COTTON TREE
Sierra Leone

In how many other cities would a tree be so cherished as to survive over two centuries of dramatic urbanization? Bravo, Freetown.

The settlement of Freetown, now capital city of Sierra Leone, was founded on 11 March 1792 by a group of formerly enslaved African-Americans who were freed in return for their loyalty to British forces during the American War of Independence. On arriving back on African soil in 1787, it is said the group held a service of thanks under a great kapok tree (*Ceiba pentandra*) growing close to the shore. The tree, now reputed to be over 500 years old, became a symbol of freedom and of the city that grew up around it.

INOSCULATION

The stems of two close-grown trees form an intimate kissing contact.

Inosculation, from the Latin *osculare*, meaning 'to kiss', is a natural phenomenon, the result of two stems, or two branches of the same or different trees, growing so closely together that they eventually merge. Arboriculturists sometimes create a forced inosculation by a technique known as pleaching.

'*A tree is beautiful, but what's more, it has a right to life; like water, the sun and the stars, it is essential. Life on earth is inconceivable without trees.*'

ANTON CHEKHOV, RUSSIAN AUTHOR AND PLAYWRIGHT (1860–1904)

An Orchard in Spring
Isidore Verheyden (1897)

Above: Traditional orchards are not treated with pesticides and soare safe places for livestock. Thus an orchard might produce not only fruit, but also hay, honey, meat, eggs and dairy.

Left: illustration by A.F. Lydon (1865).

Traditionally managed apple orchards are potential havens for a huge variety of wildlife. Their value lies not only in the huge abundance of spring blossom and the potential of windfall fruit, but because, like many fruit trees, apples tend to develop so-called veteran features such as rot holes and hollows at a relatively young age (decades instead of centuries). These features are an extremely valuable resource to insects whose grubs feed on dead wood, and to the birds, bats and other mammals that feed on those insects or use the holes as roosts and nest sites. But the words 'traditional management' are crucial here – an orchard sprayed with a cocktail of agrochemicals and harvested by ruthlessly efficient mechanical means can be as much of a wildlife desert as any other intensively exploited landscape.

BLACKTHORN
Prunus spinosa

A member of the plum family, blackthorn is used widely as a hedging plant because it grows densely in response to clipping and produces long, fiendishly sharp spines that make it highly effective as a stock barrier. It is one of the earlier blossoms to appear in spring, turning whole hedgerows white in March, as though heaped with late snow. The small, tart fruits, known as sloes, resemble oversized blueberries and are used to flavour the ruby-red liqueur, sloe gin.

JUBOKKO
Japan

In Japanese folklore, *yōkai* are a class of mischievous or malevolent supernatural beings, which take a huge variety of forms and sometimes appear at first glance to be normal people, animals or plants. A *jubokko* is a *yōkai* tree, and it is created when the soil in which a normal tree grows is soaked in human blood – usually on a battlefield. Having thus lost its innocence, the tree thirsts for more of the same and will snare unwary passers-by, pierce them and suck their blood through hollow branches.

SESSILE, IRISH OR DURMAST OAK
Quercus petraea

Above: The sessile oak copes well with thin soils, extending roots into crevices in the underlying bedrock.

Top left: Floral snow decks blackthorn hedge in March.

Bottom left: Illustration from the *Gazu Hyakki Yagyō* by Toriyama Sekien.

The national tree of Ireland actually grows as a native all across Europe and into Asia Minor and Iran. It is often one of the tallest broadleaved trees in a wood, occasionally reaching 40m (over 130ft). Its acorns have no stem and sit in tight clusters on the twigs. The scientific name *petraea* refers to the rocky ground on which this species can thrive – it often grows in higher and more exposed locations than its close relative the common, English, or pedunculate oak (*Quercus robur*). The Pontfadog oak in Wales, thought to have been the oldest oak in Great Britain when it fell in 2013 after an estimated 1,200 years, was a sessile oak.

MAGNOLIA
Magnolia spp.

The spectacular blooms of magnolia typically come in shades of pink and white.

A huge and ancient group of trees and shrubs, the magnolias were among the first insect-pollinated flowering plants. Their evolution predates that of the bees, so the early species were likely to have been pollinated by beetles. Their flowers are exquisite, but also exceptionally tough, with a perianth of robust tepals (undifferentiated petals and sepals). Often they bloom very early in the year, before the leaves are open – a characteristic that makes them popular as ornamental plants. The flowers symbolize resilience in many cultures, and different species have been adopted as emblems of North Korea, Shanghai, Houston and the US states of Louisiana and Mississippi.

RESIN

Resin seeps from a cut in a cherry branch, setting over a period of hours and days into a durable amber laquer.

Resins are substances stored as fluids in the outer cells of plants – in the case of trees, in the living layers of the bark – and exuded in response to injury. On contact with air they set into hard lacquer and thereby serve a sealing and healing function equivalent to scab formation in vertebrate animals. Some resins are strongly scented, many are highly adhesive. Substances originating from tree resin include amber, turpentine, balsam, frankincense and myrrh, and the sticky pine mastic used to flavour Greek retsina wine.

AVOND (EVENING): THE RED TREE
Piet Mondrian (c.1909)

Evening: the Red Tree is painted without the obvious colour green, and hints at Mondrian's developing interest in primary colours.

The Dutch modern artist Piet Mondrian is best known for his geometric paintings in strident primary red, blue and yellow, but early in his career he focused on more natural themes. The subject of *Evening: The Red Tree* is an apple tree, which grew in the garden of Marie Tak van Poortvliet and Jacoba van Heemskerck in the artistic community of Domburg on the Zeland coast. Tak, a prominent art collector, bought the work in 1910 but it now hangs in the Kunstmuseum on The Hague.

THE GREEN MAN

Iterations of the Green Man now appear throughout popular culture, as well as in the original, more spiritual context.

While the image of the Green Man is a familiar and ancient one, the term is relatively new, coined in 1939 by the folklorist Julia, Lady Raglan, to describe the leaf-wreathed or foliage-spewing heads in the carved wood and stonework of English churches. It is now used in a wider sense to link a diverse range of male nature deities, forest spirits, fertility gods and mythic heroes who may or may not be culturally related, including the Norse Odin, the ancient Egyptian Osiris, the Greek Dionysus, Celtic Lud, Herne the Hunter, Jack-in-the-Green, Father Christmas and Robin Hood.

BIALBERO DI CASORZO (THE CASORZO DOUBLE TREE)
Italy

Above: The Casorzo chimera is particularly striking when the epiphytic cherry blossoms in spring.

Right top: Wisps of silvagenitus cloud hang over primary rainforest in Sabah, Borneo.

Right bottom: The bottle tree stores water in its stems.

While it is no means remarkable for one tree to grow epiphytically on another (seeds are often lodged in tree crevices having been cached or transported there on the feet of birds or in their droppings), it is unusual for the epiphyte to grow as large as its host without killing it. In this case, where a cherry perches on a mulberry tree between the villages of Casorzo and Grana in Piedmont, Italy, it is likely that the cherry has established a root system that extends down through the trunk of the much older mulberry and into the ground. The symmetry and longevity of this leafy chimera has earned it 'celebri-tree' status, and it is a particular draw in spring, when the cherry bursts into blossom.

SILVAGENITUS

Where air temperatures are high enough, forests can generate their own clouds. Water vapour is created by evaporation of rainwater or condensation on leaf surfaces and by evapotranspiration of water released from pores in the leaves. These puffs of humid tree breath are known as silvagenitus.

BOTTLE TREE OR DESERT ROSE
Adenium obesum subsp. *socotranum*

With their pot-bellied squatness and improbable-looking topknots of branches bearing flourishes of bright pink flowers, the bottle trees of Socotra Island could be a creation from the mind of Dr Seuss. The species' swollen trunk and sparse, waxy foliage are an adaptation to life among the rocks and screes of stony deserts in Africa and the Arabian peninsula. Small bottle trees are sometimes grown as pot plants, but their full charisma can only be appreciated in a wild setting.

CHRIST'S THORN JUJUBE
Ziziphus spina-christi

A deep taproot makes the Christ's thorn jujube exceptionally drought resistant and it is sometimes cultivated to stabilize sandy soils in arid zones.

With a distribution centred on the Middle East but extending into east Africa and South Asia, the Christ's thorn jujube is a familiar tree of dry places, and highly valued for the nutritional and medicinal properties of its leaves and fruits. It is also claimed to be the species used to create the crown of thorns placed on Jesus Christ's head at his crucifixion. A huge and ancient specimen growing in Ein Hatzeva in central Israel is claimed to be the very tree from which the crown was made – and it may just be old enough.

DYRADS
Ancient Greece

The Hamadryad by Émile Bin (1870).

In Greek mythology, dryads were shapeshifting female spirits associated with oak trees. In later use the word was used collectively for a range of nymphs associated with forests, such as the Daphnaie (laurel nymphs), Meliae (ash tree nymphs) and Epimelides (fruit-tree nymphs) and also for the hamadryads, which were distinguished by being permanently embodied within a particular tree – the life of a hamadryad was said to be so closely associated with that of the tree, if it was felled, she would die.

THE LONE TREE OF WANAKA
New Zealand

Willows fringe much of the Lake Wanaka shoreline, but only one grows in it.

With its picture-perfect location on the edge of Lake Wanaka and the dramatic Southern Alps of New Zealand as a backdrop, it's no surprise this solitary but accessible willow has become something of an Instagram sensation. It has no official name, but is often tagged on social media as #ThatWanakaTree.

ABOVE IT ALL

The crowns of emergent rainforest trees typically support dense communities of epiphytic mosses, ferns and bromeliads.

Rainforest habitats are highly stratified. From soil and ground cover upwards, each layer has its own ecosystem, with a specialized community of other life. The uppermost of all these is the emergent layer – typically comprising trees that approach or exceed 50m (164ft) in height. These giants are relatively scarce, because reaching such great height before they are shaded over by other trees is a serious challenge. Those that make it have unfettered access to the light and are always decked in epiphytes. But they also face exposure to strong winds and intense heat. Emergent trees serve as valuable roosts and lookout points for birds, mammals and even adventurous forest ecologists, giving a clear view over many miles.

Peasant's House at Éragny
Camille Pissarro (1884)

The humble lives and homes of country folk were a lifelong source of inspiration to Pissarro.

Impressionist and Neo-impressionist painter Camille Pissarro depicted a wide range of subjects but was was a particular devotee of the French countryside. Natural scenes, he insisted in his Impressionist phase, should be painted simultaneously and holistically, ideally in one session: 'sky, water, branches, keeping everything going on an equal basis'.

Pissarro later painted this same scene in a Neo-impressionist pointillist style, in which much of the unruly vigour of the trees and hedges was lost.

FRIAR'S CRAG
England

Trees may frame the view from Friars Crag, but forests have been eliminated from most of the surrounding fells by hill sheep.

One of the most iconic vistas of the Lake District is the view from the shore of Derwent Water near Keswick, towards the long knobbly hill of Catbells, with the low rocky promontory of Friar's Crag in the foreground, with its cluster of Scots pines. The view down the lake towards Borrowdale from the crag itself is framed by the same trees, and inspired the likes of painter J.M.W. Turner, poet Robert Southey and the writer and critic John Ruskin, who described it as one of the most beautiful in Europe.

Box

Buxus sempervirens

While the vista from Box Hill now incorporates fewer trees and more roads and buildings, the topology and ecology of the hill itself are little changed since George Lambert's *Box Hill, Surrey, with Dorking in the Distance* (1733).

A compact evergreen tree of temperate and Mediterranean regions of Europe, north Africa and western Asia, box trees seldom exceed 10m (33ft) in height. Their dense form and small, even foliage means they are often grown as ornamental hedging and trimmed as topiary.

The species lends its name to Box Hill, a popular beauty spot on the North Downs of Surrey, where it grows intermingled with yew (*Taxus baccata*), forming an evergreen woodland on chalky slopes too steep to be grazed.

BANANA
(Musa acuminata)

Bananas are harvested and transported while still green, usually by sea, and ripened in specialist warehouses at their destination.

Congratulations, you have found the joker in the pack. Bananas (also known as plantains although the latter usually refers to varieties used for cooking) are the elongated berries of a small but diverse group of monocots, the Zingiberales. The plants on which they grow are not palms or even strictly speaking trees, despite often being referred to as such, because their 'trunk' is in fact a non-woody false stem made of compressed leaf bases. The word banana has an Arabic root, meaning 'finger'. In highly productive cultivars, over 200 individual fruits grow in tiers around a typical flowering stem, which can weigh 50kg (110lb) or more. The small bunches of a few to a dozen fruits in which bananas are usually sold are known in the trade as 'hands'.

YGGDRASIL

This plate, by Oluf Olufsen Bagge, appears in a 19th-century edition of *Northern Antiquities*, a selective translation of the *Edda*, first published in 1770.

O ne of the best known iterations of the global myth of the World Tree is Yggdrasil, which connects the nine worlds of Norse mythology. In the old tellings (the oldest written accounts are poems of unknown authorship referred to collectively as the *Poetic Edda*), Yggdrasil is a vast evergreen ash tree which connects the cosmos by having its branches in the heavens and its roots in various underworld springs and wells. Mythical creatures live in the tree, and the gods go about their sometimes chaotic business. The iconography of Yggdrasil has gained in popularity thanks in part to modern, big-budget screen adaptations of the sagas.

ENDANGERED PLANTS
Plymouth Pear *Pyrus cordata*

PLYMOUTH PEAR
Pyrus cordata

The Plymouth pear featured on a British stamp issued in 2009, part of a series drawing attention to endangered species.

This rare tree occurs in parts of France, Spain and Portugal and in Britain, where it is restricted to a few carefully watched-over specimens in the Plymouth area. Its celebrity appears to have been enhanced by the unholy stink of its flowers as they go over – likened to rotting scampi or wet carpet. The fruits are small, hard baubles on long stalks, but they soften at peak ripeness and carry a flavour that is recognizable as pear. The species is the only tree to be specifically protected under the UK's Wildlife and Countryside Act 1981, and because of its extreme rarity and isolation from others of its kind, seeds from the UK specimens have been deposited at Kew's Millennium Seed Bank as an insurance against local extinction.

OAK
Carry Akroyd (2012)

Oak captures the distinctive murky yellow of new oak leaves, a colour they keep only a few days before becoming flooded with green chlorophyll.

Carry Akroyd's work is familiar to many from the covers of dozens of books of nature writing. But the wordsmith with whom she is most closely associated is the 19th century 'peasant poet' John Clare, who shared Carry's home county of Northamptonshire. Clare's work demonstrates an intense love and understanding of nature, often infused with melancholy, being written at a time when working people were losing their connection to the land as a result of rural depopulation and enclosure. Carry explores similar themes in her studies of agricultural settings. *Oak* is a testament to a tree that would have stood in Clare's day, set in a landscape that has changed little between their two lifetimes. He'd be glad, if perhaps a little surprised, so find it so.

BLACK POPLAR
Populus nigra

Male catkins of black poplar provide a dash of striking colour in early spring.

The European black poplar is a lover of damp places, usually in lowlands. The name refers to its dark coloured bark and its leaves are almost triangular. Male and female catkins are borne on separate trees and resemble red and yellow fingers respectively, and the seeds that develop from the female catkins are carried by the wind on puffs of white fluff. Black poplars are widely grown as cultivars for their pale white timber, which is naturally fire resistant and was often used for floorboards. Smaller stems produced by coppicing made useful poles, pegs and basketry materials. In its wild form, however, this species is now one of the rarest native trees in Britain and most individuals now grow in isolated locations where they are unlikely to achieve pollination with others of their kind.

BURR WOOD

Burr wood is
an aberration,
caused by some
interference
with the normal
growth of a tree.

A burr is an anomalous bulge of woody growth, typically low down on a tree, that can form as a result of physical damage – such as a breakage, a cut or an insect infestation, or infection with fungus or other pathogen. Inside the burr, the orderly formation of growth rings becomes distorted, resulting in mesmerizing swirls, which are highly prized by wood crafters.

Tea
Camellia sinensis

A tea plantation in Kerala, India. The neat rows are tended by hand.

Originally a native plant of northern Myanmar (formerly Burma) and Yunnan Province in China, the tea plant is now cultivated in tropical and subtropical regions around the world. Upland areas are favoured because growth there is slower, resulting in more intense flavour. Most plants are trimmed to less than 1.5m (5ft) in height so that the fresh new leaves can be easily harvested every two to thee weeks – a selective process which, remarkably, still happens by hand.

ANTIBES IN THE MORNING
Claude Monet (1888)

Monet painted dozens of views of Antibes in 1888, claiming 'What I bring back from here, will be sweetness itself, white, pink and blue, all enveloped in a magical air'.

Despite the painting's title, the coastal city of Antibes plays definite second fiddle to the clear light of the Mediterranean and the trees placed in the foreground. Like other Impressionists, Monet loved to play with colour – we are fooled into accepting orange and yellow as the principle hues of foliage we know should be grey-green.

ESPALIER

Fruit trees like this cherry can be encouraged to fruit in surprisingly cold climates by growing in espalier form against a sheltered south-facing wall.

An espalier is a tree that has been trained into a regular, two-dimensional growth form, often against a trellis or wall. The practice is carried out for both aesthetic and practical reasons. With fruit trees, an espaliered tree is coaxed into a shape whereby no branch grows in the shade of another. Espaliers can also benefit from the shelter and residual heat of a garden wall, allowing fruit to ripen faster and avoiding frosts in marginal climates. From the gardener's point of view, additional benefits are that the tree takes up less space than a free-standing one, and the fruits are easier to pick.

THE FELLING OF DONAR'S OAK
Germany

In an etching from 1919, Pagan locals submit after Bonifatius (the latinized name for Boniface) fells their sacred oak.

Paganism was alive and well into the early Middle Ages of northern Europe, much to the chagrin of the Roman Catholic Church. The Anglo-Saxon Bishop Boniface (born Winfred of Crediton in Devon) devoted almost four decades to converting various parts of what is now Germany. On one of his missions, he and his retinue set about felling a great oak sacred to Donar, Norse god of thunder (also known as Thor) with an axe. The story goes that before the tree was completely cut through, a great wind came and finished the job. This was interpreted as divine approval, and when no answering thunderbolt came to strike him down, Boniface had little trouble converting the populace. Wood from the oak was used to build a chapel on the site, dedicated to Saint Peter.

BRIGHTON TREES
England

The exotic looking verdigris onion dome of the North Gate of Brighton's Royal Pavilion, glimpsed though some of the thousands of street and park trees in the city.

When the diarist Dr Samuel Johnson visited the seaside town of Brighton in 1777 he wrote despairingly about the lack of trees: 'The place is truly desolate and if one had a mind to hang oneself for desperation at being obliged to live there, it would be difficult to find a tree on which to fasten a rope.' These words appear to have stung the city authorities into action, and a programme of tree-planting began that has continued to this day, making Brighton one of the greenest cities in the UK.

METHUSELAH
USA

The identity and location of the world's oldest non-clonal tree of known age is strictly secret.

The traditional way to age a tree is by counting the rings in a complete trunk. In clonal species, where new trunks sprout from ancient root systems, and in species such as yew, where the trunk often rots away, this becomes impossible. However, it can be done with Great Basin bristlecone pines (*Pinus longaeva*) – immensely long-lived, non-clonal species whose slow growth allows them to survive in the dry, hostile, high-altitude habitats of California, Nevada and Utah. Methuselah, an individual living at a secret location, was accurately dated from a sample cored from its trunk in 1957 at 4,789 years, making it 4,853 in 2021. While this is the oldest non-clonal tree of precisely known age, another bristlecone pine, known as Prometheus, was cut down in 1964 in order to have its rings counted. It was 47 years older than Methuselah at the time, strongly suggesting other older specimens may exist in the region.

GLASTONBURY HOLY THORN
England

The Glastonbury thorn is said to have sprouted to life from the staff of Joseph of Arimathea.

This unusual variety of hawthorn (*Crataegus monogyna* 'Biflora') earns its religious association by blossoming twice yearly, around Easter and again at Christmas. The original, on Wearyall Hill, near the Somerset village of Glastonbury, is said to have sprouted from the staff of Joseph of Arimathea – credited variously as Jesus' uncle, as the disciple who entombed his crucified body, as founder of Christianity in Britain, and in Arthurian legend as the guardian of the Holy Grail. Holy thorns can be seen widely in the Glastonbury area and elsewhere, having been grown from cuttings grafted onto blackthorn stems to maintain their special blossoming character, which is not expressed reliably in specimens grown from seed.

EL DRAGO (DRAGO MILENARIO)
Tenerife

El Drago Milenario now stands in its own park in Icod de los Vinos, Tenerife, after a road was rerouted for its protection.

The millennium dragon tree, *Drago Milenario*, is the largest and possibly oldest living example of its species, *Dracaena draco*. It is both a national monument and a symbol of its native island of Tenerife. *El Drago* is widely reputed to be around 1,000 years old, though more conservative estimates place it at less than 400. It stands over 20m (66ft) tall with a similar measurement around the base, and when it fruits, its weight is estimated to increase by over 3 tonnes. A huge cavity in the trunk, once filled with rocks and cement in a misguided effort to strengthen it, was cleared out and now contains an extractor fan to help keep the wood dry and discourage the growth of fungi.

Seahenge (Holme I)
England

A timber monument created on low-lying marshy ground over 4000 years ago poses fascinating questions about ancient human society in what is now Britain.

During a spring walk at low tide in 1998, near the Norfolk coastal village of Holme-next-the-Sea, amateur arachnologist John Lorimer noticed the stump of a tree emerging from the beach. The stump was close to where he had recently discovered a Bronze Age axe head, so he continued to monitor it as successive tides washed away more of the sediment. A circle of split logs about 7m (23ft) in diameter was revealed, with a narrow entrance just wide enough for a person to access. In the centre of this carefully demarcated space, the stump of a large oak had been placed, upside down. Everything pointed to this being a place of

ritual significance, and dating revealed the structure had been built in the spring of 2049 BCE, when the site was a salt marsh. The timbers had been preserved by a remarkable sequence of natural changes: the marsh had flooded with fresh water; an accumulation of peat had created anaerobic conditions that prevented decay; and inundation by the sea. Once exposed to the air, the ancient wood began to deteriorate rapidly and a decision was swiftly made to excavate and remove it for preservation. It can now be seen at the Lynn Museum in Kings Lynn.

Szekeres Erzsébet varrott meseszőnyege:
Az égigérő fa
5+2Ft

MAGYAR POSTA

SZEKERES E.   1989.   FOTÓ: MOLNÁR G.

ÉGIG ÉRŐ FA (THE SKY-HIGH TREE)
Hungary

Postage stamp from Hungary depicting a tapestry of the Sky-high Tree by Erzsebet Szekeres.

In the *Táltos* folklore of Hungary, there is a tree without a top, known variously as the Tree of Life, the World Tree, or the Sky-high Tree. The tree reaches up to connect the underworld and the terrestrial realm to seven or nine layers of the sky, and the shaman-like *Táltosok* are the only people permitted to climb and experience the wonders in its branches, which include the Sun and the Moon, and extraordinary creatures including the great *Turul*, a huge mythical falcon that is a national symbol of Hungary.

PRESTON PARK ELM
England

The Preston Park 'twins' shortly before one of them sickened and had to be felled.

The city of Brighton takes pride in its trees, and none more so than an ancient English elm (*Ulmus minor* var. *vulgaris*) growing in Preston Park, one of a remarkable pair known as the Preston Twins, which beat the odds to escape Dutch elm disease for decades. Sadly the other twin did eventually succumb and had to be felled in 2019. The Twins were planted in the early 17th century, making the survivor the oldest of its kind known anywhere in the world. Brighton is also home to the National Elm Collection, with a further 17,000 specimens of various varieties planted in its streets and amenity areas.

'*We all travel the Milky Way together, trees and men.*'

JOHN MUIR, NATURALIST AND CONSERVATIONIST (1838–1914)

THE DIG TREE
Australia

A bronze panel on the Burke and Wills memorial monument in Melbourne shows the explorers by the Dig Tree.

In 1861, the four-man team of Robert Burke, William Wills, Charles Grey and John King, achieved the first south–north crossing of Australia by Europeans. However, the expedition was to end in tragedy when the party failed to return on time to their halfway depot camp on Cooper Creek in south-east Queensland. The camp party, led by William Brahe, had waited a month longer than instructed, but on 21st April, facing starvation themselves, made the agonizing decision to leave. They buried what provisions they could spare and carved the instructions 'DIG 3FT NW' on the trunk of a coolibah tree (*Eucalyptus microtheca*). In a cruel twist of fate, Burke, Wills and King arrived the same night, but by the time rescuers arrived, only King was alive to tell their story. The tragedy is compounded by the fact that both parties treated the Aboriginal people they encountered with hostility, failing to recognize that local knowledge might have saved them.

LEVENS HALL TOPIARY GARDEN
England

The art of topiary still tends to divide opinion, but the age of the garden at Levens Hall, near Kendal in the Lake District, gives it a special claim to fame.

The art of topiary – clipping dense, fine-foliage shrubs into formal or fantastical forms – dates back at least two millennia, and was a feature of Roman horticulture. It has always been somewhat controversial – Pliny the Elder disparaged it in his *Naturalis Historia*, completed in 77 CE – and while it was hugely popular in Renaissance Europe it became deeply unfashionable in the early 18th century before a revival a century later. The clipped garden of Levens Hall in Cumbria is thus remarkable in having survived the whims of fashion, and is regarded as the oldest surviving topiary garden in the world, with strange and wonderful living sculptures looking much as they did in the late 1600s.

WOLLEMIA NOBILIS
Australia

Wollemia nobilis produces flat evergreen needles on springy, often slightly drooping branches.

Known colloquially but inaccurately as the Wollemi pine, *Wollemia nobilis* is an evergreen conifer, more closely related to the monkey puzzle than any pine. It is named after the Wollemi National Park in New South Wales, Australia, where it was discovered in 1994. New species of tree are always exciting to botanists, but what captured media and public attention on this occasion was the fact that previously the genus *Wollemia* had been described only from fossils. The chance discovery was made by a group of canyoneers and the species is named after one of them, David Noble. As an amateur botanist, Noble realized that that trees he saw were something unusual. While the species has since been widely propagated and can now be bought in garden centres around the world, fewer than 100 wild specimens exist and these have become a focus of special attention during efforts to fight the increasingly frequent and severe threat from bushfires in the region.

TUNNEL OF LOVE
Ukraine

A little-used industrial railway between Klevan and the tiny village of Orzhiv in western Ukraine has become an unlikely tourist attraction. The 5km (3-mile) long 'tunnel' passes through deciduous woodland said to have been planted during the more paranoid years of the Cold War to obscure the railway from aerial or satellite cameras. The trees are trimmed by the passage of trains carrying raw materials and finished product to and from a local plywood factory, but these are occasional and the line is quiet enough to be walked safely. Largely through social media, the picturesque location has gained a reputation as a romantic backdrop for wedding photographs and selfies.

Inside Ukraine's 'tunnel of love'.

ZUIHUAI (THE GUILTY PAGODA TREE)
China

The current *zuihuai* tree in Jingshan Park, Beijing, is maintained as a symbol of people power.

On 25th April 1644, after a decade-long campaign led by Li Zicheng, Chinese peasant rebels overthrew the Emperor Chongzhen and ended 276 years of Ming Dynasty rule. The defeated emperor fled his palace in the Forbidden City in Beijing, and hanged himself from a pagoda tree (*Styphnolobium japonicum*) in the Imperial garden. The garden is now Jingshan Park, and the tree became known as the *zuihuai* or 'guilty tree'. The original is long dead and the current *zuihuai*, replanted in 1996, is one of several replacements.

GERNIKAKO ARBOLA (THE TREE OF GERNIKA)
Basque Country

The spectacular glass ceiling at the Casa de Juntas (assembly house) in Guernica, features the celebrated oak.

One of several historic assembly trees in the autonomous Basque Country in Spain, the oak that now stands in front of the Meeting House in Gernika (the Basque name for Guernica) is the fifth in a sequence held in high esteem as symbols of freedom. Local politics has been conducted under the Gernika trees since at least the 14th century but the third tree, planted in 1858, gained new significance during the Spanish Civil War. On 26th April 1937, the town, a civilian target, was heavily bombed by the German and Italian air forces, at the request of General Franco. Local volunteers formed an armed guard to defend the tree and it survived until 2004.

ELDER
Sambucus nigra

An intoxicating sight and scent of spring in full glory, elder flowers are a magnet for insects, especially hoverflies and beetles.

Avigorous pinnate-leaved tree of waysides, waste ground and the woodland understorey, elder is known for its flat sprays of creamy white, sweetly scented flowers that appear in April and May. When pollinated, these develop into bunches of small glossy black berries. Both the flowers and the berries can be used to make cordials, syrups and wine – the essences of spring and autumn respectively (but don't consume either raw as they are moderately toxic). The bark, berries and leaves can also be used to make grey, purple and yellow-green dyes. Elder wood is pale and whittles well. The smaller stems have a central core of pith that can be removed to create a hollow tube ideal for making whistles and flutes. In the *Harry Potter* stories, the immensely powerful Elder Wand is made of elder wood with a magical core of thestral hair.

THE HOWARDS END WYCH ELM
England

The house for which E.M. Forster's celebrated novel *Howards End* is named is fictional, but was based largely on Forster's own childhood home of Rooks Nest House, near Stevenage in Hertfordshire. The massive-girthed wych elm mentioned repeatedly in the novel is shown in this photograph, and an inscription on the back in Forster's hand reads 'Only record of the wych elm in *Howards End*.'

29TH APRIL

NEW BEECH LEAVES

The green of new beech leaves is one of the most dazzling of springtime colours. These tender new leaves can be eaten in the first days of opening, before they begin to accumulate the bitter-tasting tannins produced to deter leaf-eating insects and browsing animals. The flavour is similar to that of wood sorrel or apple skin, and can be captured in a woodland liqueur known as beech leaf noyau, made by infusing beech leaves with gin, brandy and sugar.

Right: A *crosh cuirn* is a simply made talisman, whose power lies in being made without tools and specifically without cutting the component wood or wool.

Left top: Perhaps the rooks of Rooks Nest House nested in the ancient wych elm.

Left bottom: Beech leaves begin to open in April and are initially fringed with downy hairs.

MANX CROSH CUIRN
Isle of Man

On the Isle of Man a centuries-old tradition is still practiced on May Eve, in which a cross (*crosh*) made of fresh *cuirn* or rowan (*Sorbus aucuparia*) wood and sheep's wool gleaned from hedges is brought into the house and hung above a doorway, replacing one made the year before. In Pagan terms, the cross represents the four cardinal directions or elements, while for Christians it is a crucifix. In either way, the *crosh* is intended to ward off evil, casting its protection over all who enter and leave. The most important aspect of these simple charms is that the rowan twigs used to make them must be broken from the tree and never cut; the taboo against cutting rowan was shared across Celtic cultures.

HAWTHORN
Crataegus monogyna

The blossom of hawthorn is sublimely beautiful, but the scent is harder to love, said to resemble both the smell of sex and the reek of decaying flesh.

The bright green leaves of hawthorn are often among the first to open in spring, but its flowers open relatively late, leading to its alternative name May blossom and the traditional warning that spring days can be unpredictably cold: 'Ne'er cast a clout 'til May is out' (a 'clout' being a cloth worn as clothing). Left to grow tall, hawthorn trees can reach a statuesque 15m (almost 50ft), but in Britain it is more familiar as a hedging plant, responding well to trimming, forming a prickly, stockproof barrier and providing superb cover for roosting and nesting birds. In autumn the fruits, known as haws, ripen to scarlet then crimson, and provide vital food for resident birds and winter migrants such as fieldfares, redwings and waxwings.

WYTHAM WOOD
England

A busy blue tit parent visiting one of hundreds of specially erected boxes in the great natural laboratory of Wytham Woods.

The ancient, 400ha (1,000-acre) Wytham Wood (pronounced 'White-am') in Oxfordshire has been owned and managed by the University of Oxford since 1942. This association has led to it becoming one of the most intensively studied patches of forest in the world, with several ecological surveys, notably those of great tits and badgers, having run for decades. It is also home to an impressive 800 species of butterflies and moths.

EUROPEAN BEECH
Fagus sylvatica

An ancient beech tree thrives at Peak District National Park, Derbyshire.

With its muscular structure, pale smooth bark, and spectacular seasonal leaf colour, the common or European beech is widely regarded as one of the world's most beautiful trees species – queen of the temperate forests where oak is king. It is also a popular hedging plant, on account of its property of marcescence, in which twigs hold on to dead leaves throughout the winter, until they are pushed off by the opening of new buds in the spring. The cathedral-like ambience of beech woodlands is a result of the pillar-like form of the trunks and the dense canopy, which shades out most smaller trees and summer ground flora, leaving a largely empty floor carpeted in fallen leaves.

PUZZLEWOOD
England

May the Fourth be with you: *Star Wars* stormtroopers invade the Forest of Dean.

It may surprise some to know that the actual location of Middle Earth from *The Lord of the Rings* is close to the village of Coleford in Gloucestershire's Forest of Dean. Author J.R.R. Tolkien lived nearby and is known to have visited the extraordinary 5ha (12 acre) Puzzlewood, with its moss-covered rocks, ancient trees, riding trails and sunlit glades. The site has been used as a filming location for dozens of blockbuster movies and hit TV shows, and thus is also the haunt of wizards and Jedi, timelords and aliens, knights and kings. It is open to the public to explore.

WYCH ELM
Ulmus glabra

Once a common and widespread tree, the wych elm has a range from Ireland to Iraq. At maturity it can exceed 30m (100ft), but such trees are now rare thanks to Dutch elm disease. Some of the best specimens grow in the city parks of Edinburgh. Elsewhere small wych elms can still be found in many woodlands and in hedgerows where they are easily mistaken for hazels. The giveaway is the leaves, which feel rough to the touch and, as with all elms, have asymmetrical bases. The flowers incorporate both male and female structures and develop into winged fruits (samaras) each bearing a single seed in the middle of the wing. These small trees usually die when they get large enough to host the beetle that carries the elm disease fungus.

BLACK ALDER
Alnus glutinosa

It is often said that alder likes to have its feet wet.

Afast-growing but relatively short-lived species favouring swampy or waterside habitats across Europe, alder lends its name to a special kind of wet woodland, alder carr (often referred to simply as 'carr'). The male and female flowers, which are both borne on the same tree, take the form of catkins and small cones, respectively. The wood of alder turns deep orange (some say blood-red) when cut, but is resistant to rot as long as it remains wet. It was therefore often the timber of choice for the construction of jetties, boats, sluice gates and even clogs.

VIRGINIA ROUND LEAF BIRCH
Carin Wagner (2020)

The Virginia round leaf birch was thought to be extinct until 1975, when a handful of specimens were found and used to propagate hundreds of others for replanting in the wild.

American artist and environmentalist Carin Wagner paints to draw attention to trees. 'It's hard to compress what I feel for any individual tree into words, it's is too enormous,' she says. 'But joy is when I am walking with the trees and surrounded by them, and painting is the work I do to honour the species that we stand to lose.' The Virginia round leaf birch (*Betula uber*) is endemic to Smyth County, Virginia, and one of the most endangered tree species in North America.

WHITEBEAM
Sorbus aria

Common whitebeam produces dense arrays of blousey white blossom, typically in May.

The name whitebeam means 'white tree' – and references the pale undersides of the leaves, which are covered in a felt of white hairs. In bud, the leaves resemble the flower buds of magnolia. They are relatively small trees, no taller than 15m (50ft), and often feature as shrubs or hedging plants. Like other well-known *Sorbus* species, whitebeams produce clusters of white flowers and red berries. Perhaps the most remarkable characteristic of whitebeams is their tendency to hybridize and evolve unique local species. In the UK alone there are more than a dozen of these, restricted to very small areas, and by definition all exceptionally rare and endangered (see The No Parking Tree on page 41 and Ley's Whitebeam on page 261).

LONDON PLANE
Platanus × acerifolia or *Platanus × hispanica*

London planes are not named for their city of origin, but for the one whose streets they began to transform over 200 years ago.

The elegant planes that line thousands of London's streets are a hybrid between two introduced species, the American sycamore (*Platanus occidentalis*) and the oriental plane (*Platanus orientalis*) – appropriate for a city in which east meets west, both geographically and culturally. The species was discovered in the mid-17th century and widely planted in the 18th. At that time, London was one of the busiest and most polluted cities on Earth, but the trees thrived, and kept their attractive appearance thanks to their tendency to exfoliate – patches of the smooth bark are dropped periodically, along with any soot or other dirt. The species is long-lived and many of the original trees survive to this day. Despite their iconic status, they are of limited value to wildlife, as they are still very new in ecological terms.

The Orcacular Oak at Dodona
Ancient Greece

Priests and
priestesses
tending sacred
trees interpreted
divine voices
heard in the
rustling of
the leaves and
perhaps in
the sounds of
wind chimes
hanging from
the branches.

An oracle was a site of communication with the classical gods. The one at Dodona in Epirus was one of the oldest and most important in ancient Greece, and was at various times used to commune with both the Titan goddess Dione, mother of Aphrodite, and with Zeus, king of the gods. It seems that over centuries the grove dwindled to just one tree, which was eventually felled by order of the Roman emperor Theodosius in an attempt to eradicate Pagan beliefs from his Christianized empire. The Dodona oak makes an appearance in the story of Jason and the Argonauts in which a branch is incorporated into the structure of his ship the *Argo*, imparting the gift of prophecy.

CHESTNUT SUNDAY
England

The mile-long avenue of horse-chestnut trees (*Aesculus hippocastanum*) in Bushy Park near Hampton Court Palace, south-west of London, was designed by the celebrated architect Sir Christopher Wren and planted in 1699. In a revived Victorian tradition, the closest Sunday to 11th May is marked as Chestnut Sunday. The trees are usually in full flower, and a parade takes place along the avenue, followed by a funfair and picnics under the trees.

FORTINGALL YEW
Scotland

A leading contender for the title of oldest tree in Britain, estimates for this specimen growing in a small churchyard in Perthshire, Scotland, range from a conservative 2,000 to an astounding 9,000 years. The tree's true age may never be known because the heartwood is long gone and the original trunk is split so far apart that the tree now resembles a small grove. A tradition was developed in the 19th century, whereby funeral processions passed through the central gap, in recognizing and reinforcing a long-held association of yews with eternal life.

NETHER
Stanley Donwood (2013)

Nether on display as street art in Bath, Somerset, in 2017.

British artist and writer Stanley Donwood is widely known for his collaboration with Thom York and the band Radiohead, whose album covers he has designed since the 1990s. Trees are recurring motifs in Donwood's art, and his spectacular painting *Nether* was used to promote the Glastonbury Music Festival in 2014 and again as the cover of the 2019 bestseller, *Underland*, by Robert Macfarlane. When asked about the image by Macfarlane, Donwood explained that *Nether* is 'the last thing you'd ever see. It's the light of a nuclear blast that has just detonated. When you look at *Nether*, you've got about 0.001 of a second of life remaining, before the flesh is melted from your bones.' A terrifying vision, although there must be many worse places to meet the moment of apocalypse than in the shade of a classic holloway.

PENJING LANDSCAPES
China

Shuihan penjing incorporates water, rocks and living plants and often includes model buildings and figures.

The Chinese art of *penjing* or *penzai* involves the creation of miniature living landscapes. It is related to the Japanese art of bonsai, in that it usually involves painstakingly cultivated trees, but is typically more complex and naturalistic, and may incorporate water features, model buildings or rocks to simulate topographical features such as mountains, boulders or crags. There are three main styles of *penjing*: *shuihan* combines water, land and trees; *shanshui* combines rocks and plants, and *shumu* makes one or more trees the focus.

ANKERWYCKE YEW
England

Henry VIII and Ann Boleyn in Windsor Forest, where hunting served as entertainment, exercise and combat training for the royal household and their guests.

A venerable yew growing on the banks of the River Thames near Windsor and thought to be 2,500 years old, was already ancient when the nearby priory of St Mary's was built in the 12th century during the reign of Henry II. But it is the ghost of another Henry, Henry VIII, which lends the tree its fame – it is said that beneath these branches he courted, and perhaps proposed, to his second wife Anne Boleyn – a marriage whose consequences included the separation of the Church of England from Rome in 1534, the Dissolution of the Monasteries and Anne's beheading for treason on 19th May 1536. The tree is also a disputed location for the signing of the Magna Carta by King John in 1215, which is also claimed by a site at Runnymede on the other side of the river.

BLUEBELL WOODS

Dappled sunshine falls through fresh green foliage in a beech wood of bluebells in England.

While bluebells grow in many parts of Europe, the dense, shimmering carpet of a classic bluebell wood is generally considered a British speciality – the UK has nearly 50 per cent of the global population. It takes a special set of circumstances for bluebells to grow in such profusion. For a start, they need time. Bluebells grow from bulbs which divide slowly to increase the size of the cluster. This means they are slow to colonize new habitats and a woodland with an extensive carpet is likely to be very old. Bluebells favour beech woods, where the dense summer canopy limits the ground flora and reduces competition from other woodland plants. Bluebells do most of their growing in early spring, before the tree canopy is complete.

MAY-SHINE

Bright rays of morning light dazzle through the fresh new leaves of a beech tree.

The term *Maienschein* (meaning 'May-shine') was originally coined in old German to describe the effect of strong spring sunlight filtered through new leaves. The feeling of well-being it elicits is undoubtedly made all the more intense by the fact that it is usually only experienced for a few days a year.

BAY WILLOW
Salix pentandra

This small, often shrubby willow is distinguished by thick, glossy leaves, which resemble those of the bay (*Laurus nobilis*) but lack the same strongly aromatic scent. In flower, however, its short catkins are clearly different from small gold cluster-blooms of true bay. Bay willows are native to northern Europe and Asia, where they favour damp or boggy ground, and so do not overlap widely with their Mediterranean namesake, except in artificial planting schemes.

GUELDER ROSE
Viburnum opulus

A small tree of the temperate and Mediterranean woodland understorey, guelder rose is an indicatior of ancient habitat. It is often planted in hedgerows and as an ornamental shrub. It produces clusters of white flowers in midsummer – the extra-large blooms on the outside of each cluster serve as signposts to pollinators but are sterile. In autumn the scarlet fruits stand out vividly. It is a big draw for wildlife, from pollinating insects to berry-eating birds.

EL ÁRBOL DEL TULE (THE TULE TREE)
Mexico

Above: An undisputed world-record beater, the colossal Tule cypress.

Top left: Bay willow tree.

Bottom left: The wild guelder rose does best in hedgerows and woodland edges.

Montezuma cypress (*Taxodium mucronatum*) growing in the Oaxaca city suburb of Santa Maria del Tule in Mexico, has the largest girth of any living tree. When last measured in 2005, it had a diameter of 11.42m (37½ft), and a circumference of 42m (138ft), thanks to the many buttresses that flare from its trunk. It is possible this vast hulk began as a multi-stemmed individual – most Montezuma cypresses develop a girth of no more than 3m (almost 10ft). *El Árbol del Tule* is undoubtedly ancient, with estimates based on growth rate agreeing closely with local Zapotec legends suggesting it was planted about 1,400 years ago, although there are claims it may be older still.

TREE: AN ACT OF DELIBERATE NOTICING
Jo Brown (2016)

Jo drew this detailed ink study as part of the 2016 Inktober Challenge, for which the prompt was simply 'Tree'.

To draw a tree from life is to give it proper attention. To make a good job you must study its structure and its many surfaces, and in doing so you notice things you haven't before.

Illustrator Jo Brown draws every day as a means of journaling nature. She says: 'This huge oak hangs over my garden. It attracts a plethora of wildlife, from acorn weevils to treecreepers, tawny owls to acorn-burying squirrels.'

Sap

Red admiral
butterflies
feed avidly on
sugar-rich liquids
such as the juices
of overripe fruit
and here, the
sap leaking
from a damaged
tree trunk.

Sap is a feature of all vascular plants – a fluid comprising an aqueous solution of compounds, including sugars made by the plant in photosynthesis, plant hormones, and other nutrient and mineral molecules taken up from soil or water, or traded with symbiotic mycorrhizal fungi. As a general rule, sap flows from roots to branches in vessels known as xylem, and from leaves to the rest of the plant in phloem. Sap can be watery, or viscous and gummy. The sugar content makes sap an attractive food source for insects, including sap-sucking bugs such as aphids and leafhoppers, while flies and butterflies that lack piercing mouthparts dab or sip sap leaking from damaged tissues.

WHITE POPLAR
Populus alba

With bark as pale as the black poplar is dark, the white poplar is also distinguished by more rounded, irregularly lobed leaves, whose pale undersides often catch the light and make the whole tree look white. More whiteness comes in late summer, when the pollinated catkins of female trees ripen into fluffy seed heads, like puffs of cotton wool, a feature which gives poplars their alternative American name of cottonwoods.

LABURNUM TUNNEL

The 55m (180ft) tunnel of laburnum is a highlight of Bodnant Garden in the Conwy Valley on the edge of Snowdonia in North Wales. The arch was commissioned in 1880 by the garden's owner and creator, the chemist and Liberal politician Henry Pochin, to a design by Edward Milner. The garden is now managed by the National Trust and is open to the public. The arch remains a spectacular annual highlight which usually flowers in the last two weeks of May.

Right: Parliamentarian soldiers interrogate Royalist locals, unaware Charles is hiding above their heads. A cartoon by John Leech from Gilbert Abbott à Beckett's *Comic History of England*, 1880.

THE ROYAL OAK
England

Top left: Pale bark, pale leaves and later, a crop of fluffy white seeds: the white popular earns its name three times over.

Bottom left: Bodnant Garden, Conwy, North Wales. The famous laburnum arch is at its best in May and June.

Following defeat in the final battle of the English Civil War at Worcester in 1651, the future king Charles II, famously spent a day hiding from Parliamentarian troops (Roundheads) in the branches of an oak tree in the grounds of Boscobel House in Shropshire. The critical role of the tree in Charles' escape, exile and eventual return to the thrones of Scotland, England and Ireland in 1660 led to it becoming a symbol of the Restoration of the Monarchy. The Royal Oak is often depicted flanked by a lion and unicorn and has given its name to countless pubs. Charles made his return to London on this day, also his 30th birthday, and the date became known as Restoration Day or Oak Apple Day. The celebrations were conflated with older traditions marking the coming of summer and involving the gathering and display of oak boughs and the wearing of sprigs of oak leaves or oak apple galls.

TIE A YELLOW RIBBON ROUND THE OLE OAK TREE
Tony Orlando and Dawn (1973)

Yellow ribbons hanging at Quincy Center, Massachusetts, for American military personal serving abroad in Iraq and Afghanistan.

This 1973 hit song was recorded by Tony Orlando and Dawn, and was written by Irwin Levine and L. Russell Brown. It tells the story of a released convict who writes to his sweetheart, asking her to give him a sign that he is welcome home. If she wants him back, she is to tie a ribbon around the tree outside her house. If he sees no ribbon, he'll understand that he should not return. The ending is a happy one though, when he sees not one, but a hundred yellow ribbons adorning the tree. Yellow tree ribbons have become a symbol of families or communities yearning for the return of those they have been missing – be they prisoners, detainees or military personnel serving far away.

COPPER BEECH
Fagus sylvatica f. *purpurea*

A copper beech tree planted by Queen Victoria in the gardens of Drummond Castle in Perthshire, Scotland.

A mutant form of common beech first recorded growing naturally in the Possenwald forest in the state of Thuringia (now part of Germany) in 1680 has given rise to a popular cultivar widely grown in parks and gardens around the world. The dark red colouring of copper beech leaves is due to production of excess anthocyanin pigments, but the leaves start green in spring and often revert to dark green in late summer. Copper beeches were introduced to Britain in the mid-18th century and appear to have been a favourite of the landscape designer Humphry Repton, featuring in many of his parkland settings.

WILD CHERRY
Prunus avium

The wild cherry is a lovely tree in all seasons. It exhibits showstopping white blossom in April, a dramatic flush of leaf colour in autumn, and glossy peeling bark in winter. In the wild it typically grows along the edges of woods, looking as though deliberately planted there, but the effect is a natural consequence of the species' liking for sunlight. Wild trees produce abundant red, yellow and black fruits, which are smaller and less sweet than cultivated varieties but still edible and excellent in pies. The wood is richly coloured and highly decorative, and popular with wood turners and cabinet makers.

Wild cherries are less sugary than cultivated ones, but still a sweet treat worth reaching for.

DEDHAM LOCK MILL
John Constable (1820)

The paintings of John Constable serve as a sad reminder of how the loss of English elms has changed the landscape.

Much of the British countryside does not appear now as it once did, even within living memory. The dwindling of hedgerows, the proliferation of urban areas, and the development of industrial, transport and energy infrastructure, are among the most visible changes since the mid-20th century, but perhaps the most poignant is the loss of the stately silhouettes of mature English elms, formerly the second most conspicuous broadleaved tree, after oaks. While not strictly native, *Ulmus procera* had formed part of the landscape of Britain since the Bronze Age, and its loss as a result of Dutch elm disease was a national tragedy. Several organizations are working on developing resistant varieties, some the result of crossbreeding, others cultivated from the few surviving trees that show varying degrees of natural resilience to infection.

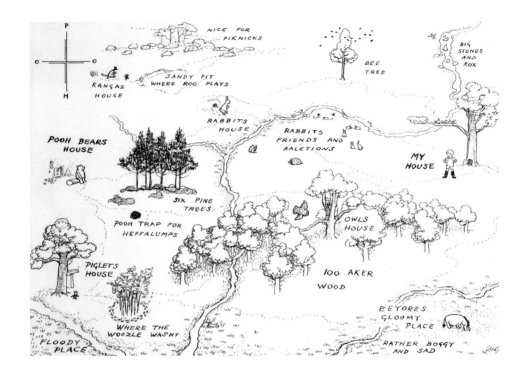

THE HUNDRED ACRE WOOD
England

E.H. Shepard's original sketches lay out a world of adventures for Christopher Robin and friends.

The setting of the celebrated *Winnie the Pooh* children's stories by A.A. Milne is based on a real place – the mixed woodland of Ashdown Forest, East Sussex, in the south of England. The wood is part of what is now the High Weald Area of Outstanding Natural Beauty. The group of Scots pines, familiar to millions from the illustrations by E.H. Shepard has changed due to reduced grazing pressure on the surrounding heathland, but there is still a special atmosphere here. It is as if Christopher Robin, Pooh, Piglet, Tigger, Owl, Eeyore, Rabbit, Kanga and Roo have just gone on an adventure and will be back for tea any time now.

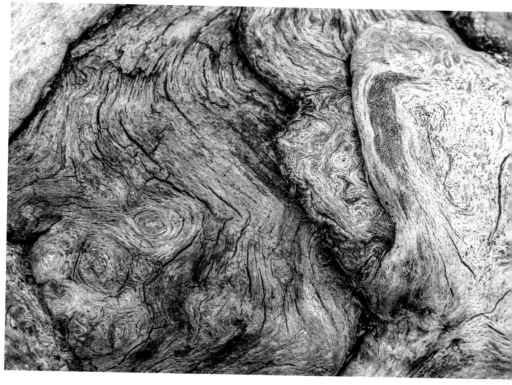

LIGNOTUBER

Burls and lignotubers are prized by woodworkers for the interesting swirls in the contorted grain.

Also known as root crowns, root collars and root burls, lignotubers are woody swellings exhibited by some trees at ground level or just below. They are usually seen in species that are routinely exposed to fire, including young cork oaks, several species of Australian eucalyptus and bloodwood, oriental camphor trees and American coast redwoods. The root collar burls of the latter are among the most massive natural woody structures known, with diameters up to 12m (39ft). A lignotuber serves as a rapid regrowth point, with a readily accessible reserve of starch which can sustain the plant until it manages to start photosynthesizing again.

VERNON OAK
England

The city of Sheffield is one of the greenest in the UK, thanks to the tens of thousands of mature trees that line its streets. A 150-year old oak in the suburb of Dore became a symbol of a battle to save thousands of these trees from unnecessary felling after the City Council signed an ill-advised deal with a private company to carry out street maintenance. Over seven years from 2012, an escalating conflict set residents, most of whom had never considered any kind of activism before, squarely against the council, contractors and police, and made news around the world. Vernon's Twitter account was used to share updates on the campaign until its successful conclusion, when a new system of tree inspections and maintenance was agreed. Vernon and thousands of other healthy trees were saved, thanks to the passion, determination and creativity of their human neighbours (see also Heartwood, page 155–156).

'*Trees are poems the earth writes upon the sky.*
We fell them down and turn them into paper, that
we may record our emptiness.'

KHALIL GIBRAN, LEBANESE AMERICAN POET (1883–1931)

MANIDOO-GIIZHIKENS OR LITTLE CEDAR SPIRIT TREE
USA

This ancient, somewhat stunted Eastern white cedar (*Thuja occidentalis*), also known as the Witch Tree, grows on Hat Point, Minnesota, overlooking Lake Superior. The site is part of the tribal lands of the Ojibwa people, to whom it is sacred and who leave offerings (traditionally of tobacco) before making journeys on the lake, in order to placate a spirit with the power to bring storms and dangerous conditions on the water. The tree is at least 300 years old and a natural bonsai, thanks to its exposed location and the lack of space afforded to its roots in the rocky outcrop.

With its roots penetrating deep into rocky crevices, the cedar spirit tree ekes out an existence, growing slowly and wisely, according to its means.

HOLLOW LOG
USA

A vast hollow log in Tulare Country in the southern Sierra Nevada has been a local landmark for at least 200 years.

No one knows exactly when this giant sequoia (*Sequoiadendron giganteum*) fell, but it was long before 1856, when the spacious hollow of its trunk was used as a base by soldiers during the Tule River Indian War. Prior to that it was already a well-known landmark and shelter used by the native Yokuts people. The log was purchased in 1885 along with the land in which it fell (now Balch Park, California), which also included a grove of standing sequoias, and it became a tourist attraction. The broken end of the log was sawn off for tidiness, and it was later bound with steel cables to improve its structural integrity. The fact that it remains intact and can still be walked on and crawled through, is testament to the extraordinary volume of wood laid down by the tree during its monumental life.

SPLIT HORNBEAM POLLARD
Hatfield Forest, England

This split
hornbeam
survives with
most of its trunk
missing because
the active xylem
and phloem
which conduct
water and
nutrients are in
the outer layers
of wood.

What appears at first to be a pair of trees growing closely side by side is in fact the split trunk of a truly ancient individual, its heartwood long rotted away. Like many trees in the ancient park landscape of Hatfield Forest in Essex, this specimen on Bush End Plain has been repeatedly pollarded (cut at around head height) to encourage vigorous new growth to sprout, despite its colossal age. Trees maintained in this manner are far less likely to become top-heavy and fall and thus live to great ages – as long, in fact, as their trunks hold out. Hatfield Forest, now managed by the National Trust and a Nature Reserve, is the most intact example of a royal hunting forest in the UK.

QUINDÍO WAX PALM
Ceroxylon quindiuense

The protective wax coating on the trunks of these stately trees was once used to make candles and soap.

The tallest species of palm tree and thus also the world's tallest monocot, the Quindío wax palm, is the national tree of Colombia, and native to montane forests in coffee-growing regions of the Andes. The tallest specimens can reach 60m (200ft), and their great height is emphasized by the relative slenderness of their trunk and complete absence of side branches.

AXEL ERLANDSON'S CIRCUS TREES
USA

In 1947, an unusual visitor attraction opened in Scotts Valley, California. The Tree Circus was the work of Swedish-American émigré horticulturalist Axel Erlandson, who used grafting and pruning to coax trees into extraordinary forms. Twenty-four of the trees now live in Gilroy Gardens Family Theme Park in California, while others have been preserved as dead wood and are displayed at the Santa Cruz Museum of Art and History and the American Visionary Art Museum in Baltimore.

The fantastical shapes of the Circus Trees in Gilroy Gardens are the result of grafting, pleaching and assiduous pruning by their creator.

LA HAYE-DE-ROUTOT YEWS
France

The cavities of ancient trees have long been regarded as places of refuge, both physically and spiritually.

Two ancient yews in the churchyard to the village of La Haye-de-Routot in north-west France are thought to be between 1,000 and 1,300 years old. Both are hollow: one contains a shrine to the Virgin Mary, the other a tiny chapel dedicated to Saint Anne. The trees came to wider attention in 2015, when one of the trees sickened and analysis of the foliage suggested it had been chemically vandalized with glyphosate. A local community group was set up to protect and celebrate the trees, which are now watched over much more closely.

'THERE IS A WILLOW GROWS ASLANT A BROOK ...'

Willows often grow directly on the banks of rivers, and the one-sidedness of their root growth means they tend to lean over the water and sometimes fall into it. This characteristic was captured in Shakespeare's *Hamlet*, where Ophelia, driven mad by the prince's rejection, falls from just such a tree and drowns, as reported by Hamlet's mother, Queen Gertrude:

'There is a willow grows aslant a brook,
That shows his hoar leaves in the glassy stream;
There with fantastic garlands did she come
Of crow-flowers, nettles, daisies, and long purples
That liberal shepherds give a grosser name,
But our cold maids do dead men's fingers call them:
There, on the pendent boughs her coronet weeds
Clambering to hang, an envious sliver broke;
When down her weedy trophies and herself
Fell in the weeping brook. Her clothes spread wide;
And, mermaid-like, awhile they bore her up:
Which time she chanted snatches of old tunes;
As one incapable of her own distress,
Or like a creature native and indued
Unto that element: but long it could not be
Till that her garments, heavy with their drink,
Pull'd the poor wretch from her melodious lay
To muddy death.'

Hamlet, ACT IV, SCENE VII, WILLIAM SHAKESPEARE (C.1599)

The scene has been painted many times, but never more exquisitely than by John Everett Millais of the Pre-Raphaelite Brotherhood, who, on discovering the backdrop location on the River Hogsmill in Surrey, complete with fallen willow, is said to have cried out, 'Look! Could anything be more perfect?'

Ophelia by Sir John Everett Millais, oil on canvas (1851–2).

THE BICYCLE TREE
Scotland

Thought to date back to the late 19th century, the tree has not suffered any ill effects from its metal addition.

This self-seeded sycamore (*Acer pseudoplatanus*) that grew up amidst a pile of scrap discarded by the village blacksmith in Brig o' Turk near Stirling in Scotland is said to have engulfed a variety of metal objects as it grew, including a ship's anchor and chain, and a bicycle. The last was hung on a branch by a local man conscripted to fight in the First World War who never returned to retrieve it. All that can be seen of the bike now are its wide vintage handlebars and part of the frame. The tree was granted protected status in 2016 for its historical and landmark significance. (See also The Hungry Tree on page 178).

TREE OF HIPPOCRATES
Greece

A large plane tree in Platia Plantanou in Kos marks the birthplace of western medical teaching.

The Greek physician and teacher Hippocrates of Kos (c.460–370 BCE) is widely regarded as the Father of Medicine. He was one of the first Western thinkers to consider disease as a natural, biological phenomenon that could be treated – rather than the will of the gods or a supernatural affliction. He delivered his teachings under a plane tree in the ancient city of Kos, in what is now known as the Platia Plantanou or Plane Square. The tree that stands on the spot now, an oriental plane (*Platanus orientalis*) is around 500 years old, and is said to be a descendant of the original. Trees grown from seeds and cuttings of this tree have been gifted around the world, and many are located in the grounds of teaching hospitals and universities including Yale and Glasgow.

BICENTENNIAL KARRI TREE
Australia

One of the world's tallest tree species, the stately karri (*Eucalyptus diversicolor*) of south-western Australia, is a keystone species of biodiverse forests. The trees seem to benefit from occasional burning, which releases nutrients locked into the deep layers of leaf litter that accumulate over time on the forest floor. Such is their resilience to fire that karri trees were often rigged for easy climbing to use as look-out points by firefighters. In 1998, to mark the Australian bicentenary, this 75m (246ft) specimen in Warren National Park, Western Australia, was fitted with 165 horizontal metal spikes, forming a spiral ladder to reach a viewing platform. It is open to all adventurous visitors ...

Intrepid tourists scale the Dave Evans Bicentennial Tree in Warren National Park, Western Australia.

Live thy Life,
Young and old,
Like yon oak,
Bright in spring,
Living gold;

Summer-rich
Then; and then
Autumn-changed
Soberer-hued
Gold again.

All his leaves
Fall'n at length,
Look, he stands,
Trunk and bough
Naked strength.

The Oak,
ALFRED, LORD TENNYSON (1889)

A mature
pedunculate oak is
a thing of splendour
in any season and
serves as a symbol
of strength in
cultures throughout
its range.

THE OAK KING
UK

An iteration of the Green Man and the archetypal horned forest god of pre-Christian European religions, the Oak King wages a cyclic battle with his alter ego the Holly King (see page 354). Oak dominates the warm, light part of the year, symbolically giving way to holly in winter.

CAESARSBOOM (CAESAR'S TREE)
Belgium

The yew tree growing next to the 14th-century gateway to the small Belgian town of Lo is considerably older than the medieval walls that once surrounded the whole settlement. Local legend has it that the Roman emperor Julius Caesar paused here on his journey to Britain in 55 CE, hitching his horses to this very tree and dozing beneath its branches. Though there is no documentary evidence that Caesar came this way, the nearby road may well date to the Roman occupation, and the tree is almost certainly old enough.

Above: A
19th-century
envisioning of
a druidic ritual.

Top left: Green
Men come in
many forms,
of which the
summer Oak
King is just one.

Bottom left:
Though the legend
behind its name
is unprovable,
this ancient
yew has Roman
era origins.

DRUIDS
Ancient Britain

The Druids were a class of priests and intellectuals that united many of
the disparate Celtic tribes of Ancient Britain. They served varied roles
as shamans, healers, spiritual leaders, teachers and keepers of oral histories.
As was common in pre-Christian Europe, the Druids regarded oak trees as
sacred components of nature, perhaps because of the myriad other forms
of life that depend on them. Even the word 'druid' is said to come from
the root words *drys*, for oak, and *wied*, meaning knowledge. British Druids
were systematically wiped out during the Roman occupation and many
of their sacred groves were destroyed, but others were incorporated into
Christian traditions and Druidism has enjoyed multiple romantic revivals
and reinventions in recent centuries.

THE HUNGRY TREE
Ireland

In the genteel park surrounding King's Inns, Dublin, a strange, inelegant spectacle is unfolding in slow motion. A relatively young London plane tree (*Platanus × hispanica*), planted no earlier than 1900, has engulfed most of the older iron bench it was presumably supposed to shade. The relatively fast-growing trunk appears to flow around the bench, which can no longer be sat upon comfortably, but has become an alternative tourist attraction.

25TH JUNE

'*As an ook cometh of a little spyr*' (*as an oak comes from a little sapling*)

GEOFFREY CHAUCER, *TROILUS AND CRISEYDE* (1374)

SUPERTREES
Singapore

Above: Singapore's unique and progressive attitude to urban nature is exemplified by its extraordinary Supertrees.

Top left: The Hungry Tree bench at King's Inns Park in Dublin, Ireland.

Bottom left: Chaucer's Troilus and Criseyde kiss on a 1995 British stamp.

An extensive urban nature park in central Singapore, known as The Gardens by the Bay, boasts multiple waterfronts, the world's largest glasshouse, an indoor cloud forest and over 100ha (247 acres) of recreational space, typically visited by more than 50 million people a year. But the features that have brought worldwide recognition and become an icon of the city state are the 18 'supertrees'. These artificial structures range from 25–50m (82–164ft) in height, incorporate vertical gardens and perform some of the same functions as real trees, providing shade by day and harvesting solar energy. At night they glow with spectacular lighting displays.

THE MAMMOTH TREE
USA

The felled trunk of the Mammoth Tree lies beside a tea pavilion erected over its cut stump. The pavilion is long gone, but the stump and the trunk can still be visited at Calaveras Big Trees State Park.

The vast trees of Calaveras Big Trees State Park in California have been wowing visitors for well over 150 years. One of them, known as the Mammoth Tree, was a 1,244-year-old, 90m (300ft) tall giant sequoia (*Sequoiadendron giganteum*) – the largest tree ever known at the time. However, at the height of the Gold Rush, this marvel of nature was seen purely as a money-making opportunity. The Mammoth was felled on 27th June 1853 following a three-week operation to sever the trunk. A year later the similar-sized Mother of the Forest met the same fate. A hotel was built nearby and parties of visitors held tea dances on the cut stump of the Mammoth Tree, while the felled trunk was used as a bowling alley. The sense of outrage over the fellings eventually began to percolate public consciousness and was a factor in the establishment of protected natural areas and the birth of the national park movement.

CUCUMBER TREE
Dendrosicyos socotranus

Cucumber trees are now protected on Socotra to curb the unsustainable practice of using their pulped trunks as emergency animal food in dry periods.

A further eccentric endemic from Yemen's isle of arboreal wonder, Socotra, (see also Bottle Tree page 87 and Dragon Blood Tree page 352), the cucumber tree is named for being part of the cucumber and pumpkin family, rather than the shape of its swollen, succulent trunk. Other species with the same common name live elsewhere.

A Price on its Crown
England

It seems a mercenary thing, to place a cash value on a tree – but doing so can be an effective means of preservation. In 2008, tree specialists in London developed a register of street trees in which specimens were valued as a means of protecting them from felling to protect other assets such as roads and buildings. The valuation process took account of size, condition, historical significance and amenity value. Several trees in the prestigious boroughs of Kensington and Chelsea and Westminster were valued at over £500,000, but those in Mayfair's Berkley Square topped the list, with one particularly large London plane (*Platanus* × *acerifolia*) valued individually at £750,000.

ASH
Fraxinus excelsior

The light, feathery foliage of the ash is unique among large European broadleaf trees.

One of the most familiar great trees of Britain and Europe, the ash is recognized by its graceful proportions, domed crown and light foliage, which moves in the slightest of breezes and casts a beautiful dappled shade. The leaves are compound, with 7–13 leaflets – all but the terminal one arranged in pairs – and they drop in autumn when they are still green. The pale, straight-grained timber is exceptionally strong, with an ability to bear huge weights and impacts, which makes it the wood of choice for tools, sports equipment, furniture and carriages. Ash wood is still used to build the frames of classic Morgan motor cars. The expected loss of more than two-thirds of all ash trees to the dieback disease caused by the fungus *Hymenoscyphus fraxineus* will have a profound impact on landscapes across its range, and nowhere more so than Britain where it is second only to oak in landscape importance.

'*A man has made at least a start on discovering the meaning of human life when he plants shade trees under which he knows full well he will never sit.*'

D. ELTON TRUEBLOOD,
AMERICAN QUAKER AND THEOLOGIAN (1900–1994)

SON AND GRANDSON OF ROYAL OAK
England

The carefully tended oaks in the grounds of Boscobel House in Shropshire are descendants of the original Charles II Royal oak.

In the years after the Restoration of the British monarchy, the oak tree near Boscobel House in Shropshire, in which Charles II purportedly hid from Roundhead troops after the Battle of Worcester in 1651 became an early tourist attraction. It died sometime in the 18th century, most likely as a result of damage caused by souvenir hunters cutting off branches. The tree now growing on the site and aged around 300 years, is said to be a direct descendant of the original (see also The Royal Oak, page 151). In an effort to ensure continuity, a third tree, grown from an acorn of the 'Son', was planted alongside by another Charles, Prince of Wales, in 2001.

NORTHERNMOST TREES

The Dahurian larch (*Larix gmelinii*) is the sole tree species growing in the world's most northerly forests, those of north-eastern Siberia. It grows as an upright tree above 72 degrees north and creeping forms continue to form part of the ground cover as the forest gives way to tundra. The northernmost examples occur at 73° 04' 32" N on the Taymyr Peninsula. In such places the growing season is reduced to around 100 days, and in winter (which lasts from late September to June), temperatures fall as low as minus 70°C (-94°F).

4TH JULY

THE FARAWAY TREE

When three children arrive in a new home on the edge of a mysterious wood, they soon embark on a series of bizarre adventures in the branches of a vast tree, populated by eccentric and magical characters. At the top of the tree, a ladder leads through a hole in the clouds to strange lands – some nice, some nasty – which move on periodically. The stories, by prolific author Enid Blyton, continue to enchant young fans more than 80 years after they were first written.

WILLOW PATTERN

Above: Spode Copeland Willow Pattern pottery.

Top left: The Yamal Peninsula in Russia boasts some of the northernmost upright trees in the world.

Bottom left: Enid Blyton's Faraway Tree books have survived updating to remain as weird and enthralling as ever.

The late 18th-century fashion for Chinese-inspired design, or Chinoiserie, in English ceramics coincided with the perfection of new techniques for mass production in the potteries of Stoke-on-Trent. Elements of the most famous blue-and-white design, now known as Willow Pattern (Blue Willow in the USA) – including the waterside garden and pavilion, fruit trees, willow, figures crossing a bridge, islands in the distance and two swallows overhead – were copied from genuine Chinese imports and used in various combinations by different potteries. The combination was first used on earthenware made by Spode in 1790, but versions were soon being widely produced and have remained hugely popular ever since. A story to accompany the design tells of doomed lovers from different social classes, who attempt to elope but are eventually captured and killed.

SYCAMORE
Acer pseudoplatanus

An imposing maple native to southern, eastern and central Europe, the sycamore has been widely introduced and naturalized elsewhere. It is planted as a shade tree, but spreads readily and this has given it a somewhat problematic reputation, especially as its fallen leaves tend to form a slippery mush that causes problems on pathways, roads and railway lines. The two-winged fruits or samaras are the inspiration for a variety of children's games, and its pale, fine-grained odourless wood is excellent for carving and for making kitchen utensils. Meanwhile, its great appeal to aphids means it makes a huge contribution to insect abundance, if not diversity, in areas where it has been introduced.

An elegant and characterful tree, the sycamore thrives in relatively moist temperate climates.

BASQUE SHEPHERDS' CARVINGS
USA

The life of a shepherd is typically an isolated one, and all the more so when the work is on the opposite side of the world from home, as it was for hundreds of Basque men who left their native Pyrenees for California and Oregon in the late 19th and early 20th centuries. Many of them developed a habit of writing or doodling on the smooth bark of aspen trees, leaving marks that darkened and swelled with time. More than 20,000 such arborglyphs have been documented, and recording them has become a matter of urgency as the trees on which they were made are now dying of old age. Many depict women and evoke the loneliness, boredom and deprivation of the shepherds' lives, sometimes poignantly, sometimes erotically.

A carved aspen trunk reflects the longings of an anonymous Basque shepherd working on Steens Mountain, Oregon, in the early 1900s.

CAJUEIRO DE PIRANGI (PIRANGI CASHEW)
Brazil

A sea of foliage all belonging to one tree, the world's largest cashew.

Driving south-east along the Avenue São Sebastião in Pirangi do Norte, Brazil, you could be forgiven for thinking you were passing a dense grove of shrubby trees. In fact almost the entire block, an area of 8,800 sq. m (almost 95,000 sq. ft) is covered by a single specimen cashew tree (*Anacardium occidentale*). The original tree has an unusually sprawling growth form, and where its lower branches have made contact with the ground they have put out roots of their own, which have then been able to sustain further outward growth. The tree is highly productive, yielding 80,000 fruits annually – inside each fleshy fruit is a familiar cashew 'nut', which is technically a seed because it lacks a nutshell.

RED RIVER GUM
Eucalyptus camaldulensis

Giant red river gums line a dry tributary of the the Darling River in outback New South Wales.

The pale, artfully peeling bark of the red river gum has helped make it an icon of the Australian outback, but it is also an ecological keystone. Groves of the species are a sign of periodic flooding, or that water is close by, even if it is not visible. Red river gums are often associated with floodplains and dry rivers, where their roots are able to tap subterranean water that seldom appears above the ground. Its branches and hollows offer homes to a range of creatures from possums to parrots, its decaying leaves help to enrich the soil, and its roots stabilize river banks, trap fertile silt and provide shelter for juvenile fish.

AERIAL ROOTS

With the aid of hundreds of aerial roots, this young and vigorous banyan will soon overcome the host tree whose structure it has borrowed for support in its early days.

An aerial root is one that passes for all or part of its length through the air rather than soil or water. Aerial roots are often adventitious, meaning that they sprout from non-root parts of the plant. In trees that begin life as epiphytes, growing on the surface of other plants, such as banyans or strangler figs, the aerial roots drop to the ground and eventually form supportive props that serve the function of a trunk.

SHAJARAT-AL-HAYAT (TREE OF LIFE)
Bahrain

The secret of the Tree of Life's fresh green appearance is a vast root system, thought to extend at least 50m (165ft) down into the sand.

Tens of thousands of visitors a year come to Jabal al-Dukhan (the Mountain of Smoke), the high point of the main island of Bahrain. They come, not just for the views, but also to see the slightly sprawling, 9.7m (32ft) Ghaf tree (*Prosopis cineraria*), which has grown nearby for well over 400 years. It is not the tree's age or stature that sets it apart, but its isolation and ability to survive so alone and so exposed in a desert where rain is a less than annual phenomenon. Local legend suggests it is a remnant of the Garden of Eden, and more recent archaeological investigation unearthed pottery and other artefacts dating back 500 years, suggesting the site has significance that predates the tree itself, and that the tree may have been deliberately cultivated.

Right: Wangarĩ
Maathai was
awarded the
Nobel Peace Prize
in 2004 for her
contributions
to sustainable
development
and democracy.

Opposite top: A
solitary Turkish
pine graces a
First World
War ANZAC
cemetery in
Gallipoli, Turkey.

Opposite bottom:
Willow Bough by
William Morris.

'*When we plant trees, we plant the seeds of
peace and seeds of hope.*'

Wangarĩ Maathai, Kenyan political and environmental
activist (1940–2011)

LONE PINE
Turkey

The Battle of Lone Pine was one of the most significant engagements involving the Australian and New Zealand Army Corps (ANZAC) during the First World War, part of their year-long campaign against the Ottoman Empire on the Gallipoli peninsula in Turkey. The battle was named for the single Turkish pine (*Pinus brutia*) that stood at the start of the battle – all others having been felled to provide timber for the construction and cover of Turkish trenches.

WILLOW BOUGH
William Morris (1887)

An enduring and popular wallpaper design, *Willow Bough* was produced by the English 19th-century designer, writer and social activist, William Morris. It is said to have been inspired by the trees overhanging the upper reaches of the River Thames near Buscot Lock in Oxfordshire, close to the village of Kelmscott where Morris lived from 1871 until 1896 when he died.

WISTMAN'S WOOD
England

Wistman's Wood, which lies high on Dartmoor in Devon, is famous for its groves of ancient, wizened trees, in particular the dwarf sessile oaks, whose growth is limited by altitude and exposure. Trees, rocks and other surfaces in and around the wood are cloaked in moss, lichen and ferns, which speak of clean air and abundant rainfall, and lend a mythic quality to the landscape.

What might elsewhere be a stately tree, on the rocky slopes of Wistman's Wood, the pedunculate oak grows slowly but surely, adopting low, twisted forms that withstand the biting wind.

NOTTINGHAMSHIRE

SHERWOOD FOREST
England

The Lincoln green cloth mentioned in some versions of the Robin Hood legend was created in a two-step process using two plant dyes: blue woad, from a herb in the mustard family; and yellow weld, made from dyer's broom.

The once vast and ancient forest of 'Shire-Wood' is a real place, but largely owes its fame to a legendary outlaw who may never have existed. This does not deter hundreds of thousands of visitors to the forest in an average year. The modern version of Robin Hood appears to be an amalgam of characters and fables, but he was already a hero in folk tales dating from the 13th century, when Sherwood covered a quarter of Nottinghamshire and spread into Derbyshire. Other early references have Hood living in Yorkshire, or in Inglewood Forest in what is now Cumbria. But the association with woodland is consistent – indeed, in some stories dating to the 16th and 17th centuries, the outlaw's name is given not as Hood, but Wood.

CENTURION
Tasmania

The Australian mountain ash (*Eucalyptus regnans*) is among the tallest tree species in the world. A specimen in the Arve Valley of Tasmania known as Centurion, vies for the title of world's tallest flowering plant with a yellow meranti in Borneo (see page 39). The most accurate method of measuring a tree's height requires a climber to drop a tape from the very top: the last time this precarious operation was performed on Centurion in 2016 it measured 99.67m (327ft). Two years later, an attempt to measure it by laser from the ground suggested it was 100.5m (almost 330ft). It's unlikely the discrepancy represents a genuine growth spurt, but it would be satisfying to see the 100m (328ft) suggested by its name. The base of the trunk was partly hollowed out by fire in 2019, but Centurion appears to be coping well with the damage.

Also known confusingly as Tasmanian oak, swamp gum and stringy gum, the Australian mountain ash is a species of eucalyptus.

Horsh Arz ar-Rabb (Forest of the Cedars of God)
Lebanon

Above: The 'Holy Valley' of Ouadi Qadisha and the Forest of the Cedars of God.

Top right: Parco dei Mostri, known locally as *Bosco Sacro* (sacred wood), Bomarzo in Viterbo, Italy.

Bottom right: The Bowthorpe Oak, in Lincolnshire, England.

The mountains that dominate the northern half of Lebanon were once extensively forested, and their trees appear to have been both venerated (see page 139) and exploited since before the beginning of recorded history. The cedars here were the raw material that allowed the Phoenicians to develop the first major seafaring and sea-trading civilization 3,000 years ago. While many more cedars have been planted, all that remains of the original old growth forest is a grove 2,000m (6,500ft) above sea level in the Qadisha Valley, in the district of Bsharri. The valley was designated a UNESCO World Heritage Site in 1998.

SACRED GROVES
Ancient Rome

The Roman term *lucus* (plural *luci*) refers to a class of woodland with special religious significance. *Luci* took the form of sacred groves or clearings, often featuring special trees and springs. They were places of celebration, communion and ritual offering. Well-documented examples include Lucus Feroniae in Etruria (now Capena in Lazio) and Lucus Pisaurensis (now the Adriatic city of Pesaro). The festival of Lucaria was celebrated within such groves on 19th and 20th July.

BOWTHORPE OAK
England

One of several English or pedunculate oaks (*Quercus robur*) thought to be more than 1,000 years old, the Bowthorpe Oak near Bourne in Lincolnshire is also one of the biggest, with a girth of 12.3m (40ft). It is also an excellent example of the south-facing tilt often exhibited by trees growing in open habitats in the temperate northern hemisphere and much appreciated by natural navigators. The trunk cavity has served as a novelty dining room and a hen house.

IL CASTAGNO DEI CENTO CAVALLI (THE CHESTNUT OF A HUNDRED HORSES)
Jean-Pierre Houël (1777)

In 1777 when it was painted by Jean-Pierre Houël, the magnificent Chestnut of a Hundred Horses appeared to contain a small building.

A European sweet chestnut (*Castanea sativa*) growing in the shadow of Mount Etna in the village of Sant'Alfio, Sicily, may be the oldest of its kind in the world, at 2,000–4,000 years old. Even more remarkable was its gargantuan girth. In 1780, close to the time it was painted by the French artist Jean-Pierre-Louis-Laurent Houël, it was measured at 190ft (a fraction under 58m). The tree's unusual name references a story in which an unnamed queen of Aragon (in modern Spain) was caught in a thunderstorm but was able to take shelter inside the tree together with her entourage of 100 knights on horseback. Today, the tree looks more like a tight grove of smaller trees, because the vast trunk has split many times, but its constituent parts remain united under the ground.

ANSTON STONES WOOD
James Brunt (2021)

The simple placement of twigs within naturally occurring voids creates dramatic transformation of decaying wood. 'Creating this piece during the COVID 19 pandemic gave me a sense of hope reaching for the sky,' says James Brunt.

Land artist James Brunt created this piece in woodland a short walk from home in Sheffield, UK, during the COVID-19 pandemic.

'It was my go-to place for exercise, dog walks and creative escape during lockdowns – the less-used pathways allowed me to find quiet spaces to stop and play and I came to know the woods really well. Spending so much time there really focused my relationship with space, and I began to notice more and more the process of life, death and decay. I was drawn to the upturned roots of fallen trees, and old stumps that, over time form interesting sculptural forms on the woodland floor.'

THIMMAMMA MARRIMANU (THIMMAMMA'S BANYAN)
India

One of many celebrated sacred banyans across India, *Thimmamma Marrimanu* is also is one of the largest trees in the world by canopy area.

Looking at first sight more like a small forest, *Thimmamma Marrimanu* near Kadiri in the Indian state of Andhra Pradesh is a single banyan tree, whose spread covers more than 19,000 sq. m (over 200,000 sq. ft). It is named after a Thimmamma, a Telugu woman who committed ritual suicide by self-immolation on the funeral pyre of her dead husband in 1433.

TEAK
Tectona grandis

The decorative archways of the Hindu Shree Swaminarayan Temple in Ahmedabad, India, are made of Burmese teak.

A tropical hardwood native to Southern and Southeast Asia, but widely introduced for cultivation elsewhere, teak has become naturalized in many tropical African countries and across the Caribbean. The wood is pale to rich yellow, with a tight grain and great strength. It is also highly valued for its natural resistance to rot and insect damage, making it suitable for construction, furniture and boatbuilding. The two largest specimens known, both exceeding 8m (26ft) in girth grow in remote areas of the Au Tuu forest reserve in the Sagaing region of Myanmar.

LIVING ROOT BRIDGES
India

A double living root bridge formed from the roots of the rubber fig by the Khasi Tribe of Meghalaya, North East India.

The small but fast-flowing rivers veining the hilly, densely forested landscapes of southern Meghalaya and Nagaland in north-eastern India are a significant obstacle to the communities that live there. Bridges are an obvious solution, but the structures created by the Khasi and Jaintia peoples are unique. They are formed from the roots of the rubber figs (*Ficus elastica*) that grow naturally on the precipitous river banks. Because the roots are part of living trees, once they are coaxed to the opposite side, they become deeply established and bridges they create are flexible, self-reinforcing and self-renewing, and may last for hundreds of years.

JOSHUA TREE
Yucca brevifolia

U2 perform
beneath a huge
silhouetted
Yucca brevifolia
during their
30th anniversary
*U2: The Joshua
Tree* tour at
Stade de France,
Paris, in 2017.

The Joshua tree is a species of yucca native to the deserts of the south-western USA and Mexico. It is particularly associated with the Mojave Desert, where its spiky form dominates the sparse vegetation. The rigidity and acute sharpness of the leaves is reflected in the Spanish name *izote de desierto*, meaning 'dagger of the desert', while for Mormon settlers it evoked the guidance of the prophet Joshua.

The species lent its name to the 1987 album by Irish rock band U2, for whom it embodied a sense of a cultural and emotional desertification. The lone tree that featured on the album artwork grew near Darwin, California, and fell in 2000. An unofficial plaque on the spot reads, 'Have you found what you're looking for?'

THE IRISH TREE ALPHABET
Katie Holten (2015)

Artist and activist Katie Holten creates tree alphabets as a means of considering new ways of communicating beyond the human. The fonts are inspired partly by the medieval ogham of Ireland (see page 67), where she grew up.

'You could say ogham is my protolanguage, my "ur-alphabet". It wasn't until I started drawing ogham characters this spring that I appreciated how organic it is. Unlike our English, which unfolds left to right and down the page, you read ogham as you would climb a tree, from the ground up.'

(*Emergence* MAGAZINE)

The Irish tree alphabet features the distinctive silhouettes of native species, so that words become copses and sentences spring up like forests. Use the alphabet to decode the dedication on page 4.

A   B   C

H   I

O   P

U   V

D E F G

J K L M N

Q R S T

W X Y Z

PLUM
Prunus domestica

The fruits of the highly productive self-fertile Victoria plum variety ripen from gold to pink to deep crimson-purple in September.

Selective breeding and cultivation have exaggerated the natural variability of this species, resulting in fruits of many colours, sizes and flavours that are known by different names: blue-black damsons, syrupy greengages, pink and gold Victorias, and small tart bullaces, which can be black or green. In the wild, plum trees often revert to a spiny growth form, showing their close relationship to the sloe-bearing blackthorn (sloe) and cherry plum.

37. — Auvers-sur-Oise — Rue Daubigny

TREE ROOTS
Vincent van Gogh (1890)

A postcard of the Rue Daubigny in Auvers-sur-Oise reveals the location of Van Gogh's last masterpiece.

The discovery in 2020 of a black-and-white photograph printed over a century earlier has helped identify the exact location in the village of Auvers-sur-Oise where Vincent van Gogh painted his last masterpiece on 29th July 1890. The painting features a steep roadside bank with exposed roots and twisted tree trunks – some of which are still present to this day. The image is of particular poignancy as the light indicates it was completed in the afternoon, just hours before the artist's death. It's difficult to reconcile the exuberance of the work with the pain that led Van Gogh to take his own life that night, and hard not to wonder what might have been if mental illness had been understood then as it is now.

LINDEN TREE ON A BASTION
Albrecht Dürer (c.1494)

Gracious and fresh-leaved after more than five hundred years, Dürer's tree portrait was ahead of its time.

The remarkable thing about this half-millennium old tree portrait is that it could have been created last week. Albrecht Dürer's naturalistic and scientific approach to nature was revolutionary in its day, and coincided with the birth of the modern sciences of botany and zoology in which plants and animals began to be meticulously observed in their own right. Previous representations of trees had been largely symbolic, but Dürer's linden could be mistaken for an illustration from a modern field guide.

THE ORIGINAL IRISH YEW
Northern Ireland

With its neat columnar form, the Florence Court yew became a favourite with tidy-minded gardeners.

The Irish yew (*Taxus baccata* 'Fastigiata') is a popular ornamental tree, cultivated widely around the world and admired for its upright, often multi-stemmed growth, which differs from the broader form of standard yews. This female specimen, growing in the grounds of Florence Court near Enniskillen, is the original. Every one of the estimated millions of Irish yews growing in gardens, parks and churchyards around the world is a clone of this tree, and all have come from cuttings rather than seed. At 250 years old, and having been cut so regularly, the Florence Court yew has a somewhat battered appearance, but it is in good health and should live for several more centuries.

THE LIGHTHOUSE TREE

Peel island on Lake Coniston was the inspiration for Arthur Ransome's Wildcat Island. A Scots pine planted to replace the original 'Lighthouse Tree' will soon emerge above the canopies of its neighbours.

On the fictional Wild Cat Island of Arthur Ransome's classic *Swallows and Amazons* (1930), the children use a tall Scots pine at the lookout point to hoist a lantern. The task of slinging a rope over the high branch falls to John Walker, the eldest of the Swallows, and his experience of the climb rings true to anyone familiar with the rough bark and snagging branch stubs typical of the species.

'The difficult moments were those when he had to pass one of the places where once upon a time there had been a bough. There was nearly always a sharp piece sticking out where the branch had been. It was easy to pass these sticking out pieces with his arms, but not so easy to get his legs over them. They were strong enough to be awkward, but not strong enough to be used as footholds.'

GENERAL SHERMAN
USA

The world's largest living tree by volume is a giant sequoia (*Sequoiadendron giganteum*) growing in the Giant Forest in Sequoia National Park in California. It zis named after the American Civil War general, William Sherman. Its current, mind-boggling dimensions include a height of 83.8m (275ft); a basal circumference of 31.3m (103ft); a basal diameter of 11.1m (36½ft); a diameter at chest height (the standard measure of tree girth) of 7.7m (25¼ft); estimated timber volume of around 1,500 cu. m (53,000 cu. ft); and an estimated total weight of around 2,000 tonnes.

General Sherman has several competitors for the title of largest tree, some growing close by in Sequoia National Park, which may overtake it in the coming years.

COMMON LINDEN OR LIME
Tilia × europaea

Tilia × europaea, generally known as the common lime or common linden, was frequently planted in parkland by the Victorians.

The common linden (or lime as it is known in the UK) is somewhat misnamed. It is a natural hybrid between the large- and small-leaved species (see pages 277 and 361 respectively) and grows wild as an uncommon woodland tree. However, it is also widely planted on streets and in parkland around the world. Like other lindens, this species has heart-shaped leaves, which are slightly lopsided at their base. White hairs on the leaf undersides in the angles between veins distinguish common lindens from others in the genus. Look also at the bark, which is ridged rather than smooth. It frequently develops large burrs, and like the small-leaved lime, you will often see clusters of twiggy shoots, or suckers, sprouting around its base. It is highly favoured by aphids, and in high summer its flowers are such a magnet for pollinating insects that whole trees can appear to be humming.

PEDUNCULATE, COMMON OR ENGLISH OAK
Quercus robur

The deeply
fissured bark of
common oaks is
easily recognized
even when the
distinctive
short-stalked,
lobed leaves are
shed in winter.

Perhaps the most loved and fêted tree in Europe, the long-lived common oak is widely claimed as a national and regional emblem and a symbol of countless businesses, charities, community groups and institutions. It is most easily distinguished from the similar sessile oak (*Quercus petraea*) by the long stalks (peduncles) of its acorns, which contrast with the short leaf stalks. In the sessile oak (see page 81), the leaves have long stems, the acorns have short ones. The scientific name *robur* references the strength of its prized timber. Where it grows as a native, this archetypal oak nurtures a spectacular diversity of other life – ecological surveys of individual specimens in British woodlands have yielded more than 400 species of insect per tree.

THE TRAIL OF THE LONESOME PINE

She Had Never Been Up There Before... a scene from John Fox's classic novel, illustrated by Frederick Coffay Yohn, depicting the central female character, June Tolliver.

The Trail of the Lonesome Pine was originally a novel by John Fox – a tale of feuding families and star-crossed lovers set in the Appalachian Mountains. It was published in 1908 and went on to become a successful stage play and film – but is perhaps best remembered for the 1913 song it inspired, and famously sung by Laurel and Hardy in their 1937 film *Way Out West*.

'In the Blue Ridge Mountains of Virginia,
On the trail of the lonesome pine –
In the pale moonshine our hearts entwine,
Where she carved her name and I carved mine;
Oh, June, like the mountains I'm blue –
Like the pine I am lonesome for you,
In the Blue Ridge Mountains of Virginia,
On the trail of the lonesome pine.'

FROM 'ON THE TRAIL OF THE LONESOME PINE',
BALLARD MACDONALD AND HARRY CARROLL (1913)

HIBAKU JUMOKO (HIROSHIMA SURVIVOR TREES)
Japan

A chilling image from the US military archives shows the aftermath of the atomic bombing of Hiroshima in 1945. Remarkably, 170 trees in the central blast zone survived.

Early in the morning of 6th August, 1945, an atomic bomb dropped by the US Air Force detonated over the Japanese city of Hiroshima. An estimated 140,000 people died in the city on that day, many more afterwards, and virtually every living thing within a 2km (1¼ mile) radius of the epicentre was incinerated. Somehow, in the months after the blast, buds emerged on the charred stems of around 170 trees in the blast zone, many of which are still living. A small organization called Green Legacy Hiroshima grows seedlings from the seeds of these remarkable parent trees, and gifts them around the world to places that have suffered natural disasters, and to nuclear nations as gestures of peace and hope. As Green Legacy co-founder Tomoko Watanabe says, 'Trees have a magical power to tell each person what they need to hear.'

Caledonian 'Granny Pines'
Scotland

An ancient Scots pine stands proud in the Caledonian forest of Glenmore in the Cairngorms National Park, Scotland.

The native forests of Scotland once covered huge areas of the Highlands, from valley bottoms to around 650m (over 2,000ft) above sea level. On high ground these comprised fairly sparse stands of Scots pine and juniper over heather, but lower down they included a wide range of broadleaved species – oak, birch, rowan and holly – and an abundant ground flora of ferns, mosses, lichens and boreal wildflowers. Areas of genuinely ancient Caledonian forest became incredibly rare throughout the 19th and 20th centuries, and truly ancient pines – known as 'grannies' – generally survived only on inaccessible crags where they were safe from grazing by sheep or deer. Restoration schemes are now underway in several areas, with fencing a crucial measure to protect regenerating tree cover.

CROFT CASTLE CHESTNUTS
England

An appealing but unsubstantiated story about the Croft Castle chestnuts says they were grown from nuts salvaged from the wrecked ships of the Spanish Armada.

This avenue of enormous Spanish or sweet chestnuts (*Castanea sativa*) in the grounds of Croft Castle near Leominster, Herefordshire, dates from between 1580 and 1680. It is said to have been planted in a formation representing the Spanish Armada, which suffered defeat to England at the Battle of Gravelines off the coast of France on this day in 1588, possibly using nuts plundered from the fleet.

JŌMON SUGI
Japan

Japan's oldest tree is a slow-grown mountain cedar whose slow and steady growth has seen it achieve monumental age.

This ancient Japanese cedar (*Cryptomeria japonica*) grows on Yakushima, one of Japan's small southern islands, within an area designated a UNESCO World Heritage Site and Biosphere Reserve. The tree was discovered in the 1960s and was a factor motivating the authorities to protect the island's pristine forests. In forestry terminology, pristine means they have never been felled. The name *Jōmon Sugi* references the Jōmon period of Japanese prehistory around 1000 BCE , roughly contemporary with the European Neolithic and Bronze Ages, and tree-ring analysis of samples from the branches suggest the tree is well over 2,000 years old.

BOAB
Adansonia gregorii

A used postage
stamp from
Australia,
depicting a
boab (2005).

The Australian boab trees, with their squat, elephantine trunks and spongy wood, are remarkable in that their close relatives, the baobabs, are all African. While other biological affinities (such as the presence of marsupials in Australia and South America) are explained by the fact that all the southern continents were once united in a landmass known as Gondwana, the boabs and baobabs are too closely related for that to be the case. Recent research suggesting that the boab is actually a relatively recent species have prompted a new theory that it may have been carried out of Africa by early humans, who valued it as a source of both food and materials. In an interview with *Australian Geographic* magazine Professor Jack Pettigrew, said 'If you were a migrant, and you thought, "What will I put in my pocket?", it would probably be baobab seeds.'

WYNDHAM PRISON TREE (HILLGROVE LOCKUP)
Australia

According to local newspaper reports from the 1930s and '40s, the hollow bole of this large boab (*Adansonia gregorii*) growing outside Wyndham, Western Australia, was used in the 1890s as a lockup for Aboriginal prisoners being taken to the town for sentencing. The 'cell' is accessed by an opening cut into the trunk and can accommodate several people. The words 'Hillgrove Police Station' were once carved into the bark of the tree, but have since been lost to decay and overwriting. While trees have certainly been widely used throughout history for chaining prisoners, there are no contemporary accounts suggesting the Hillgrove Lockup was ever actually used as a prison and it was not mentioned in a 1905 report on the mistreatment of Aboriginal prisoners in the area. This has led some historians to regard the story as a fabrication for tourists.

Wyndham Boab Prison Tree, near Wyndham, Western Australia.

ABORIGINAL SCAR TREE
Australia

The so-called 'scar trees' of Australia are living and dead trees bearing distinctive marks resulting from the partial removal of bark by Aboriginal craftsmen. In some cases the scars are hundreds of years old. Some trees also bear the marks of axes used to cut the bark to shape before it was carefully levered, all in one piece, from the tree. The size of the scar depends on the purpose the bark was required for: small ovals were cut to make traditional coolamon dishes and carrying vessels; medium-sized ones might have been for shields; and the largest pieces of bark would have formed the hulls of bark canoes. Other marks were made for spiritual or ceremonial reasons. The fact that many of these trees live on, centuries after they were scarred, is testament to the resilience of the trees and to the restraint shown by people who understood sustainability.

A gum tree bears a long scar where a huge piece of bark was removed long ago. The bark was taken all in one piece, perhaps to make a canoe.

OLD TJIKKO
Sweden

The root system of the world's oldest Norway spruce (*Picea abies*) has been radio-carbon dated to 9,562 years, and must have been one of the first to colonize the region at the end of the last Ice Age. The visible part of the tree, a slender trunk around 5m (16½ft) tall is much younger, but still draws a steady flow of visitors to Fulufjället Mountain in the Swedish province of Dalarna. Like Pando (see page 239), Old Tjikko is a clonal tree – trunks rise and eventually fall, but the root system lives on and continues to support new stems.

Sprouting from astonishingly ancient roots, the single stem of Old Tjikko stands sentry over the sparse plateau of Sweden's Fulufjället National Park.

THE BOSTON LIBERTY TREE
USA

A 19th-century engraving shows Bostonians protesting the Stamp Act gathering around the Liberty Tree. A noosed effigy of stamp agent Andrew Oliver dangles from the branches.

On 14 August 1765, a crowd gathered beneath a large elm tree on Boston Common in Boston, Massachusetts, to protest against new taxes being imposed on them via a Stamp Act passed by the British government. It was the first public act of American rebellion against the Crown. The Act was repealed, but the defiance continued, and rallies often centred on the tree; the area around it became known as Liberty Hall. When the American War of Independence broke out in 1775, Boston was placed under siege, and the tree was felled by the British, aided by colonists who remained loyal to the old country. In the centuries after independence, the site of the Liberty Tree lapsed into relative obscurity, until a new plaza was created in 2018, with a commemorative stone monument and a newly planted elm tree.

THE BIRNAM OAK
Scotland

Siward.
What wood is this?

Menteith.
The wood of Birnam.

Malcom.
Let every soldier hew him down a
bough,
And bear't before him : thereby shall
we shadow
The numbers of our host.

Act VI., Scene 3.

Above: A souvenir illustration by Henry Irving, from an 1888 production of *Macbeth* at London's Lyceum Theatre.

Right: The Birnam Oak, Birnam, Dunkeld, Perthshire, Scotland.

With its spreading branches now supported on crutches in an attempt to prevent them splitting the largely hollow trunk, the Birnam Oak in Perth and Kinross, is said to be the lone survivor of its kind (sessile oak, *Quercus petraea*) from what was once a vast forest. Thought to be well over 500 years old, it would have stood in 1599 when William Shakespeare toured the area and gained inspiration for his darkly tragic 'Scottish play'.

The increasingly unhinged Macbeth believes himself invincible because of a witches' prophecy that he is safe until Birnam Wood comes to his castle, several miles away at Dunsinane:

'THIRD WITCH: *Be lion-mettled, proud, and take no care*
Who chafes, who frets, or where conspirers are.
Macbeth shall never vanquish'd be until
Great Birnam Wood to high Dunsinane Hill
Shall come against him.

MACBETH: *That will never be*
Who can impress the forest, bid the tree
Unfix his earth-bound root? Sweet bodements! good!
Rebellion's head, rise never till the wood
Of Birnam rise, and our high-plac'd Macbeth
Shall live the lease of nature, pay his breath
To time and mortal custom. ...'

Macbeth, SCENE IV, ACT I, WILLIAM SHAKESPEARE (1606)

But as Macbeth's enemies Malcom and Macduff advance via Birnam, they order their soldiers to cut branches from the trees to use as camouflage. Thus the wood does come to Dunsinane, and the prophecy is fulfilled as Macbeth loses both his throne and his head.

The real-life Macbeth bore little resemblance to the Shakespearean character. He ruled Scotland in the 11th century and contemporary accounts describe him as brave and generous. He died on this day in 1057.

Right: This fairytale two-storey tree house is in fact a pair of chapels built into the hollow trunk of a vast and ancient oak.

Opposite top: Global tree density map.

Opposite bottom: The bark of rainbow eucalyptus is so colourful, you would be forgiven for thinking it had been spray painted.

CHÊNE CHAPELLE (THE CHAPEL OAK)
France

The pedunculate oak (*Quercus robur*) growing in the Normandy village of Allouville-Bellefosse is reputed to be the oldest in France. Local legend claims it as the site where William of Normandy acceded to his dukedom in 1035 – 31 years before he defeated the Saxon Harold Godwinson at Hastings to claim the throne of England as William the Conqueror. Even if the legends are not strictly true, the tree is at least 800 years old. The vast trunk was burned hollow by a lightning strike in the 17th century and subsequently converted into a shrine, and later, with the addition of a tower and a staircase for access, into two tiny chapels. Masses are held here twice a year.

A MAP OF TREES

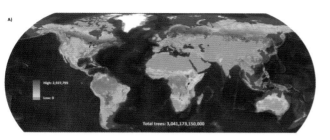

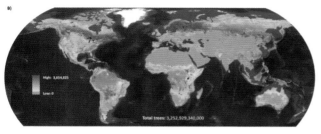

In 2015 a project involving ecologist Thomas Crowther and remote-sensing expert Henry Glick combined a variety of datasets to come up with a new map of global tree coverage and the most accurate estimate produced so far of the total number of trees on Earth. The result was considerably more than previously thought, at around 3 trillion, but this is less than half the number that were probably growing at the dawn of human civilization.

RAINBOW EUCALYPTUS
Eucalyptus deglupta

The rainbow gum or Mindanao gum has an unusual distribution for a eucalyptus – one of few to be naturally absent from Australia, its tropical range centres on the Philippines, and even reaches the northern hemisphere. Furthermore, it is the only member of its huge genus of more than 700 species that is a rainforest specialist. It's a fast-growing tree of impressive stature, regularly topping 60m (around 200ft), but its fame comes from its spectacular bark, which it sheds in strips, revealing streaks of astonishing colour.

WHITE WILLOW
Salix alba

A craftsman fits the splice in a cricket bat in a small Sussex factory in 1932.

The largest of the willows is named for its long, narrow leaves, which are pale on their undersides. Left to grow tall, white willow can reach 25m (over 80ft), but when coppiced, or pollarded, it puts on extremely rapid, multi-stemmed growth and the flexible stems, known as withies, are using in thatching and basketry. The fast-growing, straight-trunked subspecies *Salix alba* var. *caerulea* is cultivated specifically for the manufacture of cricket bats. The pale wood is straight-grained, relatively light and highly resistant to dents and splintering.

TEMPERATE RAINFOREST

Misty mountains and forest near the Troup Passage in the scenic Great Bear Rainforest, coastal British Columbia, Canada.

Rainforests are not restricted to the tropics. Temperate rainforests are a feature of areas that receive more than 1m (3¼ft) of rain a year and are generally restricted to areas where the presence of a nearby ocean exerts a moderating influence on temperatures – such places rarely get very hot or very cold. The ground flora of temperate rainforest typically comprises mosses and ferns – the diversity and abundance of flowering herbs are limited by the lack of access to direct sunlight. The trees themselves must either be shade tolerant as seedlings and saplings, or wait their turn to spring up in the gaps left by fallen predecessors.

THURINGIAN FOREST
Edvard Munch (1904)

A painful scene of environmental damage shows the red soils of Thüringer Wald in Germany bleeding away.

Best known for his rendition of howling despair in *The Scream*, Edvard Munch often used his art to convey mental turmoil. His depiction of a recently deforested valley near the sanitorium in Bad Elgersburg, where he was being treated is equally agonising, but here it is the land that is screaming. The Thuringian Mountains receive around 1m (3¼ft) of rain a year, and in this image, we see the horrific results of rain on denuded soils: unchecked erosion, slumped banks and blood-red run-off.

EL GRANDE
Australia

Surviving Australian mountain ashes or swamp gums of Tasmania's Styx Valley include many of the tallest trees in the Southern Hemisphere, but greater giants have been lost.

A sad story. *El Grande* was a landmark mountain ash (*Eucalyptus regnans*), whose celebrity status was due to its prominent position at the head of Tasmania's Derwent Valley and its huge height (79m/259ft), girth (19m/62ft) and volume (estimated at 439 cu. m/15,500 cu. ft). Taken together these statistics earned it a reputation as the world's largest angiosperm or flowering plant. The 350-year-old giant was protected from felling, but in the autumn of 2003 forestry contractors set fires to dispose of left-over branches after clear-felling nearby trees. The fire spread to the interior of *El Grande*'s trunk, which served as a flue, making the fire burn ferociously hot, and the damage was catastrophic. The entirely avoidable nature of the tragedy appalled the Australian public and shone a bright light on the unsustainable and negligent exploitation of Tasmania's old growth forests.

A Sunday on La Grande Jatte
Georges Seurat (1884)

Then, as now, the urban trees of late 19th-century Paris offered welcome relief from summer heat.

Painted on a very large canvas so the foreground figures are around life size, George Seurat's neo-impressionist masterpiece was an attempt to capture light, shade and colour in a scientific and realistic way, using tiny dots of paint that blend only in the viewer's eye. No one could claim his treatment of trees or people at leisure by the Seine is realistic – both are weirdly rigid and simplistic – but the expression of light and temperature is astonishing: from the squint-inducing glare of the sunlit areas to the sweet relief offered by the cool green shade of the trees.

ORANGE
Citrus × sinensis

Orange trees grow best in warm, frost-free climates, and rely on regular rain or irrigation.

The sweet cultivated orange tree is a hybrid between two wild species, the grapefruit-like pomelo (*Citrus maxima*) and the mandarin (*C. reticulata*). It is now the world's most widely cultivated fruit, favoured for its delicious flavour, health-giving vitamin content and the ease with which it can be transported and stored without spoiling. Orange trees are also grown as ornamentals with handsome glossy leaves, showy white blossom and luminous bauble-like fruits.

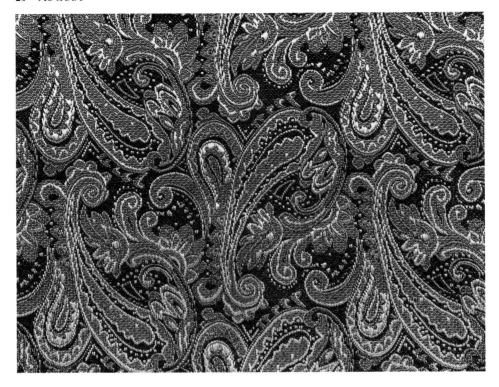

PAISLEY AND THE SACRED CYPRESS
Iran

The teardrop-shaped paisley design is also known as 'Tear of Allah'.

The popular pattern known as paisley is a variation on a Middle Eastern design. The teardrop shapes are derived from more vertical forms in Zoroasrtian art, which represented sacred cypress trees such as the Cypress of Kashmar. This sprouted from a branch delivered from paradise by the prophet Zoroaster, and was planted in the Iranian city of Kashmar. The tree was felled in 861 by order of the Caliph Al-Mutawakki' 'alà Allāh, and used in the construction of his new palace in Samarra, which stands to this day.

PANDO
USA

The famous clonal grove of quaking aspen in Utah is also known as Trembling Giant.

With a name that means 'I spread' in Latin, Pando is widely reputed to be the world's largest known organism by weight, at an estimated 6,600 tonnes. To the uninitiated, Pando appears not so much a single entity, but rather as a grove of quaking aspen (*Populus tremuloides*). But each of the roughly 40,000 stems grows from a shared root system, thought to be at least 14,000 years old, with some extreme estimates suggesting it may have been growing for almost a million years. While there are many such groves across North America, this one at Fishlake National Forest in Utah is unusually large, spreading over 43ha (107 acres).

CLOUD PRUNING

Cloud pruning is a horticultural tradition in the Far East akin to topiary, in which trees or shrubs are clipped into cloud-like forms, based loosely on their natural structure. Individual boughs are trimmed to emphasize their separateness and shaped into bulbous forms reminiscent of a fancy poodle-clip.

A tall cloud-pruned juniper makes a quirky statement in the Parc Floral de la Source, France.

KALALOCH TREE ROOT CAVE
USA

The aptly nicknamed 'Tree of Life' clings to existence on the Olympic coast of Washington State, USA.

Also known locally as the Tree of Life, this unusually formed Sitka spruce in the Olympic National Park, Washington state, has become a tourist attraction. The cliff on which it grows has been eroded by a small stream, leaving the tree suspended. Visitors are invited to marvel at the miracle of the continuing survival of a tree with its roots deprived of soil, but the truth is more prosaic – the tree has plenty of other roots, extending back into the remaining part of the cliff, and no doubt well-supplied with water by the same stream that has left it so exposed. This does not make it any less of a marvel – a wonder of arboreal tenacity.

ISLE OF THE DEAD
Arnold Böcklin (1883)

Above: In version three of Böcklin's *Isle of the Dead* (1883), the sombre journey appears to be taking place in the grey light of dawn.

Top right: The Lorax, as he was imagined in the 2012 Universal Pictures movie.

Bottom right: The *Islinger Tanzlinde* in Isling near Lichtenfels in Bavaria, Germany.

This enigmatic and unsettling image by Arnold Böcklin was so popular he painted it several times with slight differences over twenty years – the repetition making it somehow creepier, like a recurring dream. In every version, a white-clad figure is rowed towards a fortress-like island with a dense grove of dark, densely packed cypress trees – considered funerary trees in both Christian and Islamic cultures. Böcklin himself never named or explained the scene, except to hint that it came to him in a dream, but the popular interpretation is that it represents a dead soul being delivered to some kind of afterlife. The tiny island is imaginary, but resembles in part several in the Mediterranean, including Stromboliccio off Sicily.

'*I am the Lorax. I speak for the trees, for the trees have no tongues.*'

FROM *The Lorax*, DR SEUSS (1971)

31ST AUGUST

VILLAGE LINDENS
Northern Europe

In the days of the Roman Empire, in settlements throughout the Germanic lands (now Germany and much of Scandinavia) prominent linden or lime trees were typically the focus for legal proceedings, celebrations and other community gatherings. They were known as *Gerichtslinde* (court lindens), *Tanzlinde* (dance lindens) or *Dorflinde* (town or village lindens). Before Christianity arrived in Europe, lindens also carried religious significance, and were regarded as sacred to the Norse goddess Freja.

EPPING FOREST
England

Loughton Camp is one of many prehistoric settlements in Epping Forest – in this case the earthworks are Iron Age and may have been built by the local Celtic tribe, the Trinovantes.

Epping Forest, on the outskirts of London, has been a peopled landscape for millennia, with fortifications built around high points offering strategically important views. It was designated a royal hunting forest in the 12th century, but continued to offer a way of life to commoners who foraged, grazed animals and collected firewood there. It also became the haunt of outlaws and later, highwaymen, including the infamous Dick Turpin.

As Victorian London grew, so did the need for recreational green space and on public holidays the forest absorbed hundreds of thousands of visitors. This extraordinary popularity eventually lead to The Epping Forest Act of 1878, landmark legislation that protected the area from enclosure or privatisation and ensured it will remain a place for public enjoyment in perpetuity.

GOLDEN WATTLE
Acacia pycnantha

Above: A quintessentially Australian vista in New South Wales, over eucalyptus forests and golden wattle in bloom.

Right: Golden wattle flowers feature on an Australian postage stamp from the early 1970s.

This small tree is native to south-eastern Australia, though it has been planted and naturalized elsewhere. It typically grows as an understorey species. Botanically speaking, the 'leaves' are not leaves at all, but flattened leaf stems known as phyllodes, though they serve the same function. The tree was officially designated as a national emblem of Australia in the bicentennial year of 1988. The green and gold sporting colours of Australia are based on those of the golden wattle and other wattle species.

THE ORIGINAL BRAMLEY APPLE TREE
England

Malus domestica 'Bramley's Seedling' is one of the world's best-known and most prized apple varieties. The large, sour fruit are ideal for cooking and widely acknowledged as the best option for pies, crumbles and sauces. The original tree grew from a pip planted by a girl called Mary Ann Brailsford in a garden in the Nottinghamshire village of Southwell in about 1809. Apples grown from seed do not 'breed true', so each one differs in the quality of its fruit. The quality of the apples from Mary Ann's tree was recognized in 1856 by aspiring grower Henry Merryweather, then aged just 17. He took several cuttings and created the first Bramley orchard, naming the variety after Matthew Bramley, who owned the garden by that time. The original tree is now over 200 years old, and in terminal decline as a result of infection with honey fungus. It is currently being cared for by horticulturalists at Nottingham Trent University with the aim of prolonging its life for as long as possible while taking cuttings for grafting onto new trees on the nearby campus.

Domesticated apples are cultivated from grafts in order to ensure the quality of fruit can be replicated.

JUDEAN DATE PALM

Modern date palm cultivars can bear well over 100kg (220lb) of fruit in a season.

The Judean date palm, a variety of *Phoenix dactylifera*, was a symbol of the ancient kingdom of Judea where it was cultivated for thousands of years. Climate change and the devastation wreaked by centuries of regional unrest brought an end to cultivation in the Middle Ages and the celebrated ancient variety was lost. However, during the excavation of King Herod's palace at Masada in Israel in the 1960s, an ancient jar was discovered, containing superbly preserved seeds. Radio-carbon dating indicated the seeds to be between 1,900 and 2,120 years old. In 2005, a small number were germinated, and one sprouted into a tree. The tree was named Methuselah, and in 2011 it flowered, revealing itself to be male. Less ancient seeds from other locations around the Dead Sea have since been germinated, and some of the saplings are female, offering potential for this iconic tree to rise once more, like its phoenix namesake.

NEW FOREST
England

Early on a misty spring morning in the New Forest. The forest is home to ponies, deer, pigs, snakes, lizards and a host of other creatures.

The New Forest of Hampshire in the south of England was established as a National Park in 2005, but has held special status much longer than that, having been designated the *Nova Foresta* by William the Conqueror in 1079. A Forest in this original sense was a royal hunting reserve, maintained principally for deer. While large areas of the landscape are now heath and grassland, the woodlands fully deserve their reputation among the nation's finest, and are thought to contain the largest concentration of ancient trees in Western Europe, including the 500-year-old Knightwood Oak, or Queen of the Forest.

SPINDLE
Euonymus europaeus

The colourful fruit of the spindle tree ripens around the same time its leaves blush with autumn colour, and the effect is both gaudy and gorgeous.

With its candy-coloured fruits and great value to wildlife, the spindle is a popular garden tree and a valuable hedging plant. Its leaves are slightly glossy, with tiny serrations on their edges and turn deep orange in autumn. The flowers (which are borne on all specimens, spindle being a hermaphrodite species) are small and white, but the fruits are audaciously pink and ripen in early autumn to reveal bright orange seeds. Spindle spreads slowly under natural conditions and is therefore regarded as a good indicator of ancient woodland. The name comes from a common usage of the fine, pale wood, for making spindles used in spinning yarn. It also makes excellent knitting needles and pegs.

NEWTON'S APPLE TREE
England

The famous apple tree which grows in the garden of Isaac Newton's home, produces apples of a rare variety known as 'Flower of Kent'.

'… why should that apple always descend perpendicularly to the ground,' thought he to himself: occasion'd by the fall of an apple, as he sat in a contemplative mood: 'why should it not go sideways, or upwards? but constantly to the earths centre?'

This is how William Stukeley, a friend of Isaac Newton relayed the now famous story of an incident that supposedly inspired his friend to formulate his theory of gravity. The story is often regarded as apocryphal, though there are several accounts of Newton himself telling it.

Perhaps most remarkable is that a tree likely to be the one from which the apple dropped still stands in the garden of Newton's home, Woolsthorpe Manor in Lincolnshire. Thought to be approaching 400 years old, the tree has fallen twice, but both times has re-rooted and gone on to thrive once more.

SARV E-ABARKUH (THE ABARKUH CYPRESS)
Iran

The cypress is considered sacred, not least for its evergreen youthful-looking foliage and its longevity, but also for its naturally pleasing symmetry.

This veteran Mediterranean cypress (*Cupressus sempervirens*) growing the city of Abarkuh in Yazd, Iran, is thought to be around 4,500 years old. Some accounts suggest it was planted by the spiritual leader Zoroaster, although it is not known exactly when he lived (estimates range from the 5th century BCE to more than 5000 BCE). Perhaps the most remarkable feature of the tree, compared to others of similar great age, is its size and vigour. It stands around 25m (82ft) tall, with a girth of 11.5m (almost 40ft) and bears dense, healthy foliage.

DWARF BIRCH
Betula nana

A moose bull browses on dwarf birch in Alaska's open spruce forest of Denali National Park.

A specialist of high latitudes and altitudes, the low-growing dwarf birch forms extensive forests no more that waist high in Greenland, Iceland, Svalbard and across northern Canada and Eurasia. Further south it is restricted to high ground, where conditions are cool all year round. Its leaves are rounder than those of other birches, and its tough twigs have dark reddish-brown bark. It is browsed by reindeer and caribou, moose and red deer, whose clipping reduces its height even further.

THE VOICES OF TREES

The light foliage of silver birch leaves procedures fizzing colour in autumn – but how does it sound?

'I can nearly always tell what trees I am near by the sound of the wind in their leaves, though in the same tree it differs much from spring to autumn, as the leaves become of a harder and drier texture. The birches have a small, quick, high-pitched sound; so near that of falling rain that I am often deceived into thinking it really is rain, when it is only their own leaves hitting each other with a small rain-like patter. The voice of the oak leaves is also rather high-pitched, though lower than that of birch. Chestnut leaves in a mild breeze sound much more deliberate; a sort of slow slither. Nearly all trees in gentle wind have a pleasant sound.'

GERTRUDE JEKYLL, VISUALLY IMPAIRED GARDEN DESIGNER (1843–1933)

SURVIVOR TREE
USA

The Survivor Tree flourishing again close to its former home in the 9/11 Memorial Plaza, New York.

When the twin towers of the World Trade Center collapsed following the terrorist attacks of 11 September 2001, a Callery pear tree (*Pyrus calleryana*) planted over 20 years earlier was damaged and buried for weeks in the rubble. But as the massive and painstaking process of clearing the site progressed that autumn, workers noticed that somehow one branch of the tree was putting out new leaves. Despite its ordeal, the tree seemed determined to live. It was carefully transferred to a tree nursery in the Bronx, where it spent nine years putting on healthy new growth. In 2010 it was relocated again, to the 9/11 Memorial Plaza, where it stands today as a symbol of resilience.

Pyrus Malus L.

CRAB APPLE
Malus sylvestris

A hand-coloured copperplate botanical engraving of the familiar crab apple by Jan Christiaan Sepp, 1796.

The ancestor of domestic apples is a small- to medium-sized tree, common across Eurasia. It bears small, hard fruits, rarely more than 3cm (1¼in) in diameter. Crab apples are intensely tart in flavour, but sweeten when cooked, and make excellent jellies and jams because they contain large quantities of the setting agent pectin. They are often grown in orchards, not for their fruit, but because their long flowering period makes them a reliable source of pollen for fertilizing the main crop. Crab apples have a rich folklore, and are widely associated with love and marriage.

SILVER BIRCH
Betula pendula

The whiteness of birch bark is a result of light reflecting off crystals of the betulin, an organic compound with a variety of potentially valuable pharmacological properties.

A dauntless pioneer species, birch is sometimes regarded as little more than an arboreal weed by foresters. But this view neglects the fact that birch is the natural forest cover across vast swathes of northern Europe and Asia. In older English texts it is referred to simply as birch or *birk*, and the prefix 'silver' appears to have been coined by the poet Alfred, Lord Tennyson. Birch wood serves a wide variety of structural purposes and is often the favoured fuel for smokehouses. Its peelable bark can be used as an alternative to paper and as tinder, and the fine branches are used for making the besom brooms no self-respecting witch or wizard would be without.

MANGROVE FOREST

As well as describing a group of coastal trees with exceptional tolerance for inundation with salt water, the word 'mangrove' is also used to refer to the habitats created by these trees – a kind of coastal, tropical swamp-forest. Mangroves are crucially important habitats, rich in marine life, but also providing secure roosting and nesting sites for birds, and nursery areas for fish and reptiles, including crocodiles. Their dense growth also protects vast stretches of coastline from erosion and catastrophic battering by storm waves.

EUROPEAN HORSE-CHESTNUT
Aesculus hippocastanum

This statuesque native of the Balkan Peninsula has been widely introduced to the rest of Europe and North America. Children know it as the conker tree, and its glossy and irresistibly pocketable fruits are among the most popular playthings provided by nature. The trees are at their most spectacular in flower, when they are covered with candle-like spires of white (in some varieties bright pink) blooms.

HAZEL
Corylus avellana

Fast-growing hazel can be identified by its snaggle-toothed leaves, smooth grey bark, yellow spring catkins (the male flowers) and clusters of nuts with ruffs of ragged bracts. It is relatively short-lived, unless it is occasionally coppiced (cut back at ground level), a practice that promotes vigorous regrowth. Done repeatedly, coppicing can render the tree virtually immortal. Coppicing rotations vary from one or two years for flexible whips and poles, to decades for stout poles, firewood, charcoal and nuts. The dense matrix of stems and potentially heavy nut crops promoted by coppicing make for excellent wildlife habitat.

Above: A wattle fence woven from springy coppiced hazel stems provides a sturdy barrier, while simultaneously protecting and sheltering a new hedge growing up around it.

Top left: The waters around mangrove roots are warm, sheltered and safe from predators, thus teem with life.

Bottom left: The glowing treasure of a fresh conker in its jewelbox case.

DA VINCI'S RULE OF BRANCHING

The meticulous studies of nature recorded by artist and polymath Leonardo da Vinci continue to provide food for thought for specialists in many fields of study. Da Vinci's observations of trees included several general rules for growth and form, the best known of which concerns the fractal nature of branching.

He wrote that 'all the branches of a tree at every stage of its height when put together are equal in thickness to the trunk'. It's a simple enough theory, and it appears to hold true for virtually all kinds of tree, from the first branching of the trunk to the very finest twigs, though proving it for mature specimens with potentially thousands of branchings is intensely labour-intensive and time-consuming.

However, computer modelling has offered a convincing answer to the question of why trees of all species seem to grow this way. The mode of growth appears to be the one that offers best resilience to strong winds, making a tree as strong as it reasonably needs to be without wasting energy to lay down any excess wood.

Da Vinci studied trees meticulously. In this sketch from around 1480, he focused on the effect of light falling on foliage.

LEY'S WHITEBEAM
Sorbus leyana

Ley's whitebeam puts on an explosive display of seasonal colour in autumn. Its fruits are eaten and dispersed by birds.

One of several Critically Endangered species of whitebeam with incredibly limited natural ranges, the Ley's whitebeam was discovered in 1896 by parson-naturalist Reverend Augustin Ley. Considered the rarest tree in Wales, it is thought to be a hybrid between the rowan (*Sorbus aucuparia*) and another scarce whitebeam species, either rock whitebeam (*Sorbus rupicola*) or grey whitebeam (*S. porrigentiformis*). The handful of specimens living in the wild grow clinging to rocky outcrops in the Brecon Beacons. It is thought they are slow to reproduce naturally and highly susceptible to grazing, so only survive on crags that can't be easily accessed by sheep. A further population has been established at the National Botanic Garden in Wales as a safeguard against extinction, which may be their natural fate otherwise.

SWAMP CYPRESS KNEES

A distinctive feature of wetland habitats in the southeastern USA, swamp cypresses are also planted as ornamental trees, as here in the Magnolia Plantation in Charleston, South Carolina.

The trunks of swamp-growing cypresses, such as *Taxodium distichum*, are often heavily flared or buttressed to provide stability in soft, saturated ground. Perhaps the most distinctive features of this species and its close relatives are their 'knees' – knobbly, woody growths that sprout directly upwards from the roots into the air above, around the main trunk. It used to be assumed that these knees served the same function as the aerial roots or pneumatophores of mangroves, but current thinking invokes a more multifunctional role, including further stabilization and the trapping of sediment and other material to reinforce the ground in which the tree is rooted.

ROCKY MOUNTAIN WATERFALL
Albert Bierstadt (1898)

Painted late in Bierstadt's career, *Rocky Mountain Waterfall* is unapologetically grandiose and brimming with the light and romance that always marked his studies of the region.

Albert Bierstadt was an explorer-painter – one of the first European artists to travel into the American west and particularly the Rocky Mountains. He devoted 30 years of his career to bringing their grandeur to the wider world, and achieved enormous success before falling out of fashion and critical favour, as artists often do. His work was unashamedly romantic, often extravagant in scale, and arguably overblown: for example the dwarfing of the firs in the middle distance and background of this image suggest a cascade of truly colossal proportions. However, the Bierstadt legacy has since been re-evaluated in the light of the positive role it played in the birth of the American Conservation Movement.

WESTERN HEMLOCK
Tsuga heterophylla

Dense stands of western hemlock line the banks of Fish Creek, near Juneau, Alaska. Trees that occasionally fall into the river create temporary leaky dams, which help slow the flow – a valuable form of natural flood management.

A tall, drooping conifer widely planted as a timber crop and an ornamental tree, the western hemlock is native to western North America. Its evergreen needles are soft and very dark green, except when freshly grown in spring at the tips of the branches, when they start out bright, almost luminous green. Each needle has two narrow white lines on its underside. The cones are small with thin scales. This is not the toxic hemlock famous for killing Socrates – that is a herbaceous plant (*Conium maculatum*) in the umbellifer or carrot family, but the shared name reflects a similar scent to the foliage of both plants.

THE BISHNOI SACRIFICE
India

A Bishnoi woman prays at a Khejri or ghaf tree in Rajasthan, India, where it is now the official state tree.

Khejri trees (*Prosopis cineraria*), known elsewhere as jammi or ghaf trees, are iconic species of desert regions of South Asia and the Middle East (see Shajarat-al-Hayat, page 193). Their ecological, cultural and religious importance is such that in 1730, a Bishnoi Hindu woman called Amrita Devi and her three daughters laid down their lives to try and prevent the felling of their local trees to make way for a new palace for the Maharaja. Far from subduing the protest, the violence meted out by the Maharaja's men lead to a greater uprising, in which 363 Bishnoi died for their trees.

WONDERBOOM
South Africa

The *Wonderboom* in Pretoria (the name is Afrikaans for 'Wonder Tree') was so-named by Dutch-speaking settlers who encountered its welcome shade as they migrated east from the British-ruled Cape Colony in 1836. They realized that what appeared at first to be a grove of the native fig (*Ficus salicifolia*), 50m (164ft) across was in fact a single specimen, the branches of which had drooped and taken root where they had made contact with the ground, forming three rings of daughters around a central bole. The oldest parts of the tree are thought to date back more than 1,000 years. The grove and its surroundings were declared a nature reserve on 23 September 1988.

The Wonderboom Reserve, in easy reach of central Pretoria, has been a popular picnic and walking spot for over 150 years.

FIELD MAPLE
Acer campestre

Despite its name, the field maple is an ideal urban tree, well suited to hedging, and surprisingly tolerant of pollution.

The field maple is a modest-sized tree, often found in hedgerows where it copes well with trimming, and is widely planted as an ornamental species within and beyond its mainly European and Mediterranean range. The leaves have five lobes, with more rounded margins than those of most other maples, and are notably smaller than sycamore leaves. The fruits are two-winged samaras. In mature trees the bark becomes thick and corky, with deep fissures. Field maple wood is very hard, with an attractive golden hue, and is often used for making musical instruments.

JUNIPER
Juniperus communis

Juniper 'berries' are widely used as a spice and famously provide the flavouring for gin (from the Dutch *jenever*).

A hardy member of the cedar family, common juniper often grows to the treeline across its vast northern hemisphere range. Juniper can be identified by its small, prickly, wintergreen needles, which grow in threes around a ridged twig, each bearing a silvery central band. Male and female cones are produced on separate plants. The male plants release copious yellow pollen in early spring. Successfully pollinated female cones swell to berry-like structures resembling miniature sloes or blueberries when ripe, but which can be easily distinguished by a mark that resembles a three-pointed star. At a time when early Christians sought to defend themselves from witchcraft, the aromatic branches of juniper were brought indoors or burned on auspicious occasions such as Hogmanay (31 December) in Scotland and Walpurgis Night (30 April) in Northern Europe and Scandinavia, the eve of May Day, when witches and evil spirit were thought to be at large.

STARA MASLINA (СТАРА МАСЛИНА)
Montenegro

Local people in Stari Bar, Montenegro, often choose to have their marriage blessed beneath the branches of the city's oldest resident.

Visitors to the suburb of Tomba in the Adriatic coastal city of Bar in the small Balkan nation of Montenegro can't help but notice its main natural attraction – a colossal olive tree (*Olea europaea*), said to be over 2,000 years old. Now surrounded by protective stonework and a fence, the tree has suffered severe fire damage but seems be thriving nonetheless, and can be observed up close for a small fee.

AMERICAN CHESTNUT
Castanea dentata

The scientific name *dentata* refers to the saw-toothed edges of the American chestnut leaves. Here, the spiky fruits are seen swelling alongside the remains of the male catkins.

This magnificent species was once a dominant presence in woodlands across the eastern USA, but was devastated by disease in the early 20th century. Up to four billion trees succumbed to blight caused by *Cryphonectria parasitica*, a bark fungus introduced from Asia. The species is currently regarded as functionally extinct in its native range, because while the root systems and stumps of some trees remain alive, any shoots they put out become infected and die before they are able to reproduce. The future of the species may depend on a variety of measures including biological control of the virus that infects the fungus and development of blight-resistant trees. The latter might happen through selective breeding, cross-breeding with closely related species from China, or genetic modification.

PEAR
Pyrus communis

The cultivated pear is thought to have been developed from a wild tree, which is regarded by some as separate species (*Pyrus pyraster*), while others regard the wild and cultivated varieties as subspecies (*P. communis pyraster* and *P. communis communis* respectively). To add to the confusion, cultivated varieties of pear grow wild in many parts of the wild pear's range, as well as in gardens and orchards. But there is small chance of mistaking their fruits – those of the wild pear are small, hard and inedible, though the Neolithic people who first began to cultivate them in various parts of Europe must have seen merit in doing so. Documentary evidence suggests that pear trees were common in Anglo-Saxon Britain, and they are frequently referred to in Norman records as boundary markers.

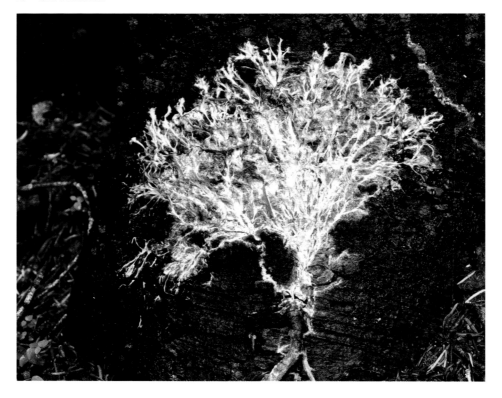

THE WOOD WIDE WEB

A spreading mat of mycelial threads (hyphae) creates a satisfyingly arboreal form – perhaps the fungi are trying to tell us something?

Mycorrhizae are mutually beneficial associations between fungi and plants. The term 'mycorrhiza' was coined in the 19th century by the German botanist Albert Bernhard Frank, but science has only recently begun to grapple with their true scale and importance. Mycorrhizae are mostly made up of mycelia – networks of microscopic threads, which are mostly invisible to the naked eye, but so long-lived and extensive that they include the world's oldest and largest organisms. The networks connect the roots of living plants, tapping them for food while simultaneously performing vital roles in plant nutrition and ecosystem health, providing a means for trees and other plants to share and acquire nutrients and to communicate using a range of chemical and electrical signals.

KRUMMHOLZ

The distinctive 'flag trees' of southern Tierra del Fuego are the result of almost constant driving wind.

Krummholz trees are those found close to the latitudinal and altitudinal treelines of subarctic and subalpine habitats, where conditions are close to the limits of cold and exposure that any tree can survive. The name is usually applied exclusively to conifers, but includes a variety of species of pine, spruce and fir, and is also known as tuckamore and elfinwood. Krummholz trees typically exhibit stunted, twisted growth forms shaped by icy wind.

BIRKENWALD I (BIRCH FOREST I)
Gustav Klimt (1902)

Klimt captured both the glow and the gloom of the north Alpine birch woods around Lake Attersee.

The Austrian symbolist painter Gustav Klimt spent several summers at Attersee, a vast lake east of Salzburg, where he produced an extensive series of landscapes featuring the turquoise lake and its densely wooded hinterland. These forest paintings are celebrated for their striking colour and depth of focus – Klimt is thought to have used a telescope to ensure that even trees in the far background were given the same detailed treatment as those to the front. Such was his obsession with the forests that locals nicknamed him *Waldschrat* or 'forest demon'.

DOUGLAS FIR
Reelig Glen, Scotland

Originally planted for timber, groves of Douglas fir have become landmarks in several parts of Scotland.

The tallest trees in the UK are Douglas firs (*Pseudotsuga menziesii*), several of which have exceeded 60m (nearly 200ft), and the current record holder, a giant growing in Reeling Glen near Inverness was last measured at 64m (210ft). Known as Big Douglas or *Dùghall Mòr* ('big dark stranger' in Gaelic), the tree is part of a planting scheme started in the early 19th century by the Fraser family, who owned the glen for five centuries before selling to the Forestry Commission in 1949. Douglas firs were prized for their massive straight trunks – one of Big Doug's neighbours was used as a mast for Robert Falcon Scott's Antarctic exploration vessel *Discovery* in 1901.

GOATS IN TREES
Morocco

Goats demonstrate their natural agility by climbing argan trees to reach the oily fruits.

The gnarled and sprawling branches of Moroccan argan trees (*Argania spinosa*) produce small fruits resembling shrunken olives. The nuts inside the fruits are the source of a valuable oil used in cooking and in hair- and skin-conditioning treatments. However, it is not the fruit or the oil that make these trees so popular with tourists, but the goats perching nonchalantly high in the branches. The animals enjoy the bitter flesh of the argan fruits, while the nuts pass through their digestive system unscathed, to be deposited in droppings below the trees, where they are collected for processing. Local farmers have recognized an opportunity to make money twice over, by gathering the processed nuts and charging tourists to take photographs. Some have been criticized by animal welfare groups for encouraging ever more goats to gather in their trees.

LARGE-LEAVED LINDEN OR LIME
Tilia platyphyllos

A grand old large-leaved lime tree beginning to develop the first glow of autumn colour.

Unlike the small-leaved and common lindens (see page 361 and 216), this species does not generally produce suckers. Large-leaved lindens are relatively scarce in the wild and thus limit the natural occurrence of the hybrid common linden. The leaves are 6–12cm (2¼–4¾in) long, with hairy undersides, and the bark is dark grey, smooth and flaky. Like other lindens, the large-leaved is hugely important to insect life, attracting vast numbers of pollinators and often teeming with aphids, whose honeydew droppings coat the leaves and anything left under the tree for more than a few hours.

THE MULBERRY TREE IN AUTUMN
Vincent van Gogh (1889)

Van Gogh painted mulberry trees on more than one occasion, but was particularly satisfied by this dazzling attempt, featuring a tree growing in the garden of the Saint-Paul-de-Mausole asylum (a former monastery) in Saint-Rémy-de-Provence. Van Gogh spent a year in the hospital following a bout of madness in 1888 during which he fought with fellow artist Paul Gauguin and mutilated his own ear. His time at Saint-Rémy was exceptionally productive, resulting in around 150 canvases, though he continued to struggle with the illness that would lead to his suicide in July 1890 at the age of 37, just as his genius was beginning to be recognized by the wider art world (see also page 211).

Despite the turbulence caused by his illness, Van Gogh found release in his art, and wrote to his brother that this painting pleased him more than most.

GINKO OR MAIDENHAIR TREE
Ginkgo biloba

Above: Turn this leaf upsidedown to see how the ginkgo gets its pubic alternative name, maidenhair.

Top left: Lombardy poplars are named for the Italian province where they are so conspicuous.

Bottom left: Ripe walnuts erupt from their pithy green fruits.

The ginkgo is the sole survivor of an entire division of plants known as the Ginkgophyta. Fossil evidence suggests the species is over 270 million years old. Individual trees are long-lived, often exceeding 1,000 years. The fan-shaped leaves are highly distinctive, with veins that spread out from the stalk, occasionally bifurcating. Many leaves develop a notch on the outer edge, thereby forming the two lobes described in the scientific name. They turn bright yellow in autumn and tend to fall very suddenly, sometimes within a single day. Ginkgos are dioecious, with male trees producing small cones and mature females laden with 'fruits' that superficially resemble cherries. The fleshy seedcoat smells unappealingly of vomit when ripe, but the nut inside is edible. Despite many health claims for extracts of ginkgo, beneficial effects are at best mild and unreliable, and undesirable side effects are common.

WAYFARING TREE
Viburnum lantana

The fruits of wayfaring tree are poisonous to humans but provide an important food source for overwintering birds.

A low-growing tree or shrub of hedgerows and woodlands, especially on chalky soils, the wayfaring tree has wrinkled oval leaves with finely serrated edges and hairy undersides. Its flowers are white clusters in spring but the species is arguably most striking when its fruits ripen from bright red to black – for a while there are berries of both colours in a cluster. At harvest times in the past, the new shoots of the recent summer's growth were long and flexible enough to be used as baler twine. Slightly older stems dry very stiff and strong, making them suitable as arrow shafts.

TREE OF KNOWLEDGE OR TREE OF IMMORTALITY

Adam and Eve by
Lucas Cranach
the Elder, oil on
panel (1526).

The Tree of Knowledge is major motif in all three major Abrahamic religions, in whose creation stories it grows in the garden where Adam and Eve are forbidden from touching it or tasting its fruit. Of course they do so, egged on in the Judaeo-Christian version by a serpent and in the Islamic telling by Satan himself, with a promise of immortality. In eating the fruit, they commit the first sin, and are banished, setting all of future humanity on its flawed and complex earthly path.

HYPERION AND THE GIANTS
USA

A true land of giants, the coast redwood forests of California boast several of the world's tallest living trees.

A giant among giants, a coast redwood (*Sequoia sempervirens*) known as Hyperion is thought to be the world's tallest tree, and hence our tallest fellow Earthling. Hyperion is named after one of the Titans, the gigantic children of Gaia and Uranus, the Earth Mother and Sky god of Greek mythology. Its precise location within California's Redwood National and State Parks complex is not publicized, but two of its near neighbours (named Helios and Icarus) are currently the second and third tallest of their kind. In 2006 Hyperion measured 115.9m (just over 380ft) and is thought to be growing slowly at 3.9cm (1½in) a year. Based on current growth rates, it will probably be overtaken in 2031 by a tree growing in the Humboldt Redwoods State Park. Known as Paradox, this upstart has grown almost 19cm (7½in) a year since 1995 and is currently fifth tallest in the world.

HOW TO MEASURE A TREE

The author's son measures a fine old oak tree. The distance over the ground between tree and observer is approximately equal to the tree's height.

One reliable means to measure the height of a standing tree is to find a straight stick whose length is the same as that from your palm to your eye, when your arm is held out straight in front of you. Grasp the stick at one end and walk away from the tree until its full height appears to match the length of the stick, held upright at arm's length in front of you. Measure or pace the distance over the ground from this point to the base of the tree – this is a good approximation of the tree's height. More precise – but more dangerous – is to drop a tape measure from the top (see page 199).

THE VALUE OF A TREE

As any nature lover knows, the real worth of a tree cannot be measured in monetary terms. As we plant ever more young trees but fail to prevent the felling of irreplaceable mature specimens, the words of early American nature writer and conservationist Susan Fenimore Cooper ring true, 170 years after they were written.

'Independently of their market price in dollars and cents, the trees have other values; they are connected in many ways with the civilisations of a country; they have their importance in an intellectual and in a moral sense. After the first rude stage of progress is past in a new country – when shelter and food have been provided – people begin to collect the conveniences and pleasures of a permanent home about their dwellings, and then the farmer generally sets out a few trees before his door. This is very desirable, but it is only the first step in the track; something more is needed; the preservation of fine trees, already standing, marks a farther progress, and this point we have not yet reached. It frequently happens that the same man who yesterday planted some half dozen branchless saplings before his door, will to-day cut down a noble elm, or oak, only a few rods from his house, an object which was itself a hundred-fold more beautiful than any other in his possession.'

FROM *Rural Hours*,
SUSAN FENIMORE COOPER (1850)

BURNHAM BEECHES
England

Morgan Freeman on set at Burnham Beeches for *Robin Hood: Prince of Thieves* (1991).

This celebrated woodland on the Chiltern Hills of south-east England is truly ancient. It is best known for its huge beeches, whose smooth trunks and massive boughs create the impression of a living cathedral. The site is owned by the City of London and the trees are managed using the traditional technique of pollarding, which allows them to achieve great longevity. The proximity of such timeless woodland to the city and to some major film studios makes them a popular filming location: scenes for *Robin Hood Prince of Thieves*, *The Princess Bride* and parts of the Harry Potter franchise were created here.

SERVICE TREE
Sorbus domestica

Historical references suggest this, the true service tree, was once much more common and cultivated than it is now across its European range. It is now considered rare or endangered almost everywhere, and especially in Britain, where it is one of our rarest trees. A single individual growing in the Wyre Forest, the so-called Whitty Pear, which died in a forest fire in 1862, was the only know specimen in the UK until small populations were discovered growing on inaccessible cliff faces in South Wales, Gloucestershire and in Cornwall.

The fruits, which resemble tiny apples or pears depending on the variety, are hard and gritty and tart, but sweeten dramatically when allowed to 'blet' or overripen. In Ancient Greece they were pickled, and in parts of Europe they are still gathered to make a cider or perry-like beverage.

The hard, marble-sized fruits of the true service tree, or Whitty pear.

BAUCIS AND PHILEMON

A delightful illustration by Arthur Rackham, shows Philemon and Baucis in their gracious and mutually entwined afterlife – he an oak, she a linden.

In a story first written down by the classical poet Ovid, which has been retold in many variations since, Baucis and Philemon were an elderly couple who, despite being poor, were the only people to offer hospitality to two strangers visiting their town. Unbeknown to the mortals, the travellers were gods travelling in disguise – Zeus and Hermes in the Greek mythology, Jupiter and Mercury in the Roman version. The gods rewarded their hosts by saving them when they destroyed the town and its selfish inhabitants by flood, and making them custodians of a beautiful temple on the site of their humble home. They also granted the couple their wish to never be parted and to die on the same day, after which they were turned into two intertwining trees, an oak and a linden (lime).

CUBBINGTON PEAR
England

Until 2011, this huge, graciously proportioned pear tree standing on a field boundary near the village of Cubbington in Warwickshire was a minor local landmark. Thought to be around 250 years old and the second largest of its kind in the UK, the tree was particularly lovely in spring when its mass of white blossom resembled a heavy fall of snow. It came to much wider public attention as a result of efforts to save it from felling as land was cleared for the controversial high-speed railway, HS2. It was voted English Tree of the Year in 2015, and described by the local Wildlife Trust as a poster-tree for all those threatened by the HS2 project. Despite several years of protests and a petition that gathered 20,000 signatures, the tree was cut down on 20 October 2020. Dozens of cuttings were taken from the tree for planting nearby, and at least some have so far survived.

EUROPEAN LARCH
Larix decidua

Conifers aren't often known for their colour being mostly evergreen, but the deciduous larch fairly dazzles in autumn.

Unusually among conifers, larches are deciduous, shedding their short soft needles in winter and growing new ones in a burst of astringent green in spring. Larches are monoecious, with male and female flowers produced on the same tree, male ones on the underside of the shoots, and female ones, sometimes called 'larch roses' at the tips. The female flowers develop into small cones, whose seeds are sought enthusiastically by squirrels and finches. Dramatic colour changes from spring green to autumn gold make larches stand out in otherwise evergreen conifer plantations.

THE GIANT HAND OF VYRNWY
Wales

When a gigantic Douglas fir on the Lake Vyrnwy Estate in Powys, Wales was damaged in a storm, it had to be felled. The tree had previously shared the distinction of being the joint tallest in Britain at 63.7m (209ft), and so rather than cutting it off at ground level, an imaginative plan was hatched to create a new landmark. Foresters cut the tree at the point it was damaged, leaving a 15m (49ft) stump, which chainsaw artist Simon O'Rourke then carved into a vast hand – symbolizing the tree once more reaching for the sky.

The stump of the massive Vyrnwy fir was given a new lease of life as art, carved *in situ* by Simon O'Rourke.

23ʀᴅ OCTOBER

I think that I shall never see
A poem lovely as a tree.

A tree whose hungry mouth is prest
Against the earth's sweet flowing breast;

A tree that looks at God all day,
And lifts her leafy arms to pray;

A tree that may in Summer wear
A nest of robins in her hair;

Upon whose bosom snow has lain;
Who intimately lives with rain.

Poems are made by fools like me,
But only God can make a tree.

Trees, Jᴏʏᴄᴇ Kɪʟᴍᴇʀ (1913)

THE SUNLAND BAOBAB
South Africa

The baobab has a wide trunk for its height, but even so, the hollow inside the Sunland Baobab is huge.

Acolossal African baobab (*Adansonia digitata*) at Sunland Farm near Modjadjiskloof in Limpopo Province, South Africa, has a total circumference of 47m (154ft), including its buttresses, and a trunk diameter of 10.64m (almost 35ft). Carbon dating suggests it is over 1,000 years old. A natural cavity in the trunk was cleared of compost in 1993 revealing artefacts suggesting it had been visited over its long life by San bushmen and early Dutch settlers. The trunk was large enough to accommodate a small bar and wine cellar, and comfortably able to admit 15 people, with almost 4m (13ft) of headroom. Parts of the trunk fell away in 2016 and 2017, but the tree lives on.

AUTUMN LEAF PIGMENT

The withdrawal of chlorophyll at summer's end allows other pigments to show their colours.

The often dramatic change in leaf colour exhibited in autumn by many deciduous trees reflects changes in the pigments present in the foliage. The maple leaves shown here appear green in summer thanks to the pigment chlorphyll. This is the chemical responsible for gathering sunlight to power the process of photosynthesis, in which water and carbon dioxide are converted into sugar and oxygen. The yellows, oranges and golds are produced by a family of pigments knows as carotenoids – these are also present in the leaves in summer but the colour is masked by the intense green of the abundant chlorophyll. Only when chlorophyll levels decline are the warm colours of the carotenoids revealed. Red and purple colouration is the result of a third group of pigments, known as anthocyanins, synthesized in response to changes in sap chemistry as autumn progresses. The production of anthocyanins is sensitive to sunlight, and so the intensity of autumn colour in a given area or year varies with the prevailing weather.

Right: The 800-year-old oak trunk near the Diana Memorial Playground is home to dozens of elves, gnomes, fairies, witches and woodland animals.

Opposite top: Odysseus half carries, half drags his stupfied crew from the land of the *lotophagi*, where they have been intoxicated by the fruit of the lotus tree.

Opposite bottom: Spotting the hundreds of creatures in the trunk of the artificial Tree of Life helps visitors to Disney World Florida pass the time while queuing to visit the Animal Kingdom theatre.

THE ELFIN OAK
Kensington Gardens, London

This hollow oak trunk from an ancient tree that formerly grew in Richmond Park was moved to Kensington Gardens in 1928. Artist Ivor Innes carved out and painted dozens of little figures into the gnarled wood, as though they inhabited it, and his wife Elsie wrote a book telling their whimsical stories. Innes continued maintaining the tree and its cast of characters as long as he lived, but the sculpture deteriorated after his death. It was restored in 1996 thanks to an appeal led by the comic actor Spike Milligan, who also helped repaint some of the figures. The tree is now contained in a metal cage to protect it from damage.

LOTUS TREE
Ziziphus lotus

A low-growing, evergreen member of the buckthorn family, the lotus tree produces polished-looking oval leaves and golden fruits that resemble tiny plums. In its mythical form, it dominated an island or peninsula visited by Odysseus, and was consumed by the native *lotophagi* or 'lotus-eaters', in whom it induced a state of indulgent and apathetic stupor leading them to forget everything that was important to them.

DISNEY TREE OF LIFE
USA

At the centre of Disney's Animal Kingdom Theme Park at Walt Disney World in Florida is an island, and on the island a tree, of sorts. Part sculpture, part landscaping, part 428-seater movie theatre, the baobab-inspired Tree of Life features more than 300 species of living and extinct animals carved and modelled into its trunk and 8,000-plus branches. The structure is built from a repurposed oil rig.

AMERICAN QUAKING ASPEN
Populus tremuloides

Above: American aspen blaze in autumn colours at Grand Teton National Park, Wyoming.

Top right: A sacred fig at the heart of the Mahabodhi temple complex.

Bottom right: This ancient yew is said to make morbid prophesies on All Hallows Eve.

The quaking aspen has the largest natural distribution across North America of any tree, growing from Alaska and northern Canada all the way to New Mexico, though in southern parts it is restricted to higher altitudes. Like its close relative the Eurasian aspen, it is known for the shimmering movement of its leaves, which turn rich gold in the fall. It reproduces readily by suckering and can thus form huge groves of genetically identical clones (see page 239). The species is also the defining feature of aspen parkland, a transitional biome between prairie and boreal forest, which covers large swathes of Canada and the northern contiguous US.

THE MAHABODHI TREE
India

The sacred fig currently growing at the Mahabodhi Temple at Bodh Gaya in Bihar, India, represents the one under which Gautama Buddha gained enlightenment in around 500 BCE. The temple around the original tree was constructed by the Emperor Ashoka who reigned between c.265 and 238 BCE, a devoted follower of the Buddha's teachings. The tree has been replaced several times, most recently in 1881, by British archaeologist Alexander Cunningham.

LLANGERNYW YEW
Wales

The huge yew growing in the churchyard of St Digain in Llangernyw, North Wales, is estimated to be more than 4,000 years old, though, like most ancient specimens of its kind, its trunk hollowed and split many centuries ago, making accurate dating difficult. Braver residents of the parish gather near the tree each Halloween, when it is said a ghostly apparition, the *Angelystor* or Recording Angel, will appear and announce the names of those who will die in the coming year.

EURASIAN ASPEN
Populus tremula

Eurasian or quaking aspen has a vast natural range, from Iceland and the British Isles in the west to Kamchatka in the east.

This much-loved tree of cool temperate parts of Europe and Asia is dioecious, with male and female catkins appearing on different trees in spring. The pollinated flowers give rise to seeds with fluffy parachutes that can carry many miles on the wind. Aspens also reproduce by suckering, where new shoots appear from underground buds on the roots or stem of the tree. The aspen owes its Latin name and character to the long, flattened and flexible stems, or petioles, to which the round, irregular-edged leaves are attached, and on which they dance in the lightest of breezes. This shimmering movement and the accompanying sound is linked in various mythologies to the faerie or spirit worlds, and crowns of aspen are said to have been laid in Celtic burials to ease passage to the underworld.

CELTIC CROSS OF LARCH
Co. Donegal, Ireland

The Celtic Cross symbol originated in the British Isles in the early Middle Ages and became a popular motif in Celtic Insular art.

In autumn 2016, passengers flying into Derry Airport in Northern Ireland noticed a startling new landmark – a vast golden Celtic cross in a forest in the Lagan Valley of Co. Donegal. The design comprises 3,000 or so Japanese larch trees (*Larix kaempferi*), which, unlike the surrounding evergreens, turn gold in autumn. It has been identified as the work of local forester Liam Emery, who planted the plot in the early 2000s but sadly didn't live to see his creation mature.

It's not the first time larches have been used in such a way. In 1992 a mapping survey of forest in the German state of Brandenburg revealed a giant swastika thought to have been planted in the 1930s to celebrate Adolf Hitler's birthday, then forgotten about. It was removed in 2000.

LiDAR Tree Imaging

LiDAR scanning technology can be used to analyse the structure of individual trees, or as here to investigate the topography of whole landscapes.

Specialists studying tree structure have long struggled with the phenomenal fractal complexity of growth forms – the more you look at a tree, the more detail is revealed. Now, however, a laser technology known as LiDAR (Light detection and ranging) is coming to their aid. The technique involves a ring of scanners placed around a tree to record the details of its structure in extraordinary detail. Computer models generated from the resulting data provide information such as the exact volume of wood in the tree, and the total length and number of its branchings. What LiDAR cannot do is provide similar detail for the equally important and arguably more intricate part of the tree which lies underground.

THORN TREE WARNINGS

While trees cannot evade the attention of hungry herbivores completely, their strategies to minimize the damage include a form of chemical communication.

The first scientific evidence that trees communicate with each other chemically came from a study of African thorn trees (*Vachellia* spp., formerly *Acacia*) growing on the savannas of East Africa. Researchers noticed that giraffes (whose immensely long tongues allow them to feed on the trees despite the presence of protective thorns) always move upwind from one tree to another, and usually skip a few trees before beginning to feed again. This, it transpired, is to circumvent another defensive tactic. When a thorn tree is nibbled, it boosts the concentration of bitter-tasting tannins in its leaves, so the browser will only feed for a short time before moving on. The injured tree also releases ethylene gas, which is detected by its neighbours (especially those downwind), and in response to this 'chemical scream' these trees will ramp up their own production, and thus gain advanced protection.

THE TRILLION TREE CAMPAIGN

Planted in the right place, trees have the potential to sequester vast quantities of atmospheric carbon. Other advantages may include flood mitigation, erosion control, pollution management and biodiversity gains.

Following his 2015 estimate of global tree population at around 3 trillion (see page 231), ecologist and campaigner Thomas Crowther calculated that the planet has room for a further 1.2 trillion trees, without losing any of the land area needed for production or other ecosystems. Furthermore, these additional trees could absorb vast quantities of carbon dioxide, dwarfing all the carbon capture technologies thus far proposed to mitigate climate change. The challenge has been taken up by youth-led

organization Plant-for-the-Planet, as an extension of the Billion Tree Campaign launched by the UN in 2006. The new target is ambitious, but with 15 billion trees already planted (2 billion in India alone), and governments, private companies and communities around the world pledging to pitch in, the trillion tree goal is achievable.

AUTUMN AFTERNOON, THE WISSAHICKON
Thomas Moran (1864)

The Wissahickon
Creek flows into
the Schuylkill
River at
Philadelphia.
Much of its length
is protected as a
Natural Landmark,
not least because
of this painting.

This idyllic vista, painted not far from the rapidly industrializing city of Philadelphia during the upheaval of the American Civil War, shows not a hint of either. Instead, Thomas Moran focused on natural beauty and drama. The air is still and clear, colours are in their peak glory and placid cattle sip crystal waters. It was a nostaligic scene before the paint was even dry, but Moran remained deeply proud of it, and rightly so.

SCOTS PINE
Pinus sylvestris

Scots pine is a pioneer species, but its natural ability to colonize cleared ground is limited by grazing pressure.

With a vast natural range extending east from Ireland across Eurasia to eastern China and south from Northern Scandinavia to Turkey, this distinctive and hardy conifer is far from exclusively Scottish. Elsewhere it is known variously as Baltic pine, Mongolian pine, Riga pine, and among foresters it is usually referred to as European redwood. The only pine native to the British Isles, it can usually be identified by its habit of shedding lower branches as it grows, its flaky, fissured bark, which is grey near the bottom but often warm russet higher up, and its needles, which are slightly twisted and borne in pairs. The cones are reddish-brown, with stout scales bearing a rounded nub on their outer surface.

DICOTILEDONI.   Tav. 685.   Cedrelee. (Brow.)
Meliacee. (Juss.)

MAOGANO o Magogano d'America.
SWIETENIA mahogoni. (Linn.)

Turpin dis.   Corsi inc.

MAHOGANY
Swietenia spp.

Genuine mahogany is a name given to the beautiful, fine-grained and lustrous red-hued timber of three species of *Swietenia* tree, all native to Central and South America and the Caribbean. The name is also applied to African species such as *Khaya anthotheca* (the original or true *m'oganwo* for which other 'mahoganies' are named), and with less justification, other than a similarity in the wood, to Chinese, Indian, Indonesian and New Zealand species. The *Swietenia* mahoganies are all threatened with overexploitation, and much of the timber currently exported from native forests is the result of illegal logging. Mahogany is the national tree of both Honduras and Belize.

WOLDGATE WOODS, 6 & 9 NOVEMBER
David Hockney (2006)

Hockney's
painting of
Woldgate Wood
formed part of a
major exhibition,
A Bigger Picture,
in 2012.

Trees are a long-term fascination for Yorkshire born artist David Hockney. During the 1990s and 2000s he spent spend several seasons painting the chalk landscapes of the Yorkshire Wolds, including a whole series the woods along Woldgate, a Roman road known by a Viking name. He returned repeatedly to Woldgate Woods, photographing and painting it in all seasons, sometimes with traditional paint, sometimes using an iPad – one of the first fine artists to do so.

WILD SERVICE TREE
Sorbus torminalis

The leaves of wild service are both lobed and toothed, and turn rich gold in autumn.

A once well-known tree whose small brown fruits (known in English as 'chequers') were considered a sweet treat after the first frosts of winter had softened them, the wild service has faded from public recognition and dwindled in abundance. It is considered an indicator of ancient woodlands because is spreads mainly by suckering, but it was also traditionally planted in the gardens of houses and inns (*Chequers* remains a common house and pub name), where the fruit was collected for consumption at home, for sale or to flavour alcoholic beverages. See also the service tree (*Sorbus domestica*) on page 291.

WE ARE MAKING A NEW WORLD
Paul Nash (1918)

Nash's devastating portrayal of a polluted and mangled no-mans-land that was woodland set the human tragedy of war in its environmental context.

What became the most famous work by Paul Nash was based on a sketch created in the devastation of Inverness Copse, near Ypres, on the Western Front of World War I during the Battle of Passchendaele. Nash was appalled, not only by the human experience of war, but by the destruction wrought on the natural world. In a letter to his wife in 1917 he wrote:

I am a messenger who will bring back word from the men who are fighting to those who want the war to go on for ever. Feeble, inarticulate, will be my message, but it will have a bitter truth, and may it burn their lousy souls.

The painting was initially published untitled as a piece of official war art, but the later addition of its bitterly accusatory title gave it a very different meaning.

315

SAPWOOD AND HEARTWOOD

The sapwood of this recently sawn pedunculate oak is clearly visible as a slighty darker layer under the bark. The paler wood in the centre is heartwood.

New wood is laid down by trees as they grow and it is formed from tightly packed vessels known as xylem. These are made of living cells, whose walls are reinforced with a complex organic polymer called lignin – one of the toughest compounds in biology. The vessels are the tree's plumbing – they conduct sap from roots to branches and leaves. New wood is made on the outside of the tree, and as the years go by old layers of growth are overlaid by new ones. Eventually their sap stops flowing and in many species the wood dies, but in doing so, it may also become more resilient to rot. Often, this so-called heartwood or duramen is a slightly different colour than the outer sapwood, or alburnum. Because heartwood is dead, however, the tree can survive perfectly well without it, and veteran trees can live for centuries with a completely hollow trunk.

WOOD ON THE DOWNS
Paul Nash (1930)

Paul Nash spent much of his childhood in Buckinghamshire, and the spare, sculptural quality of the downland landscape and its towering beech woods remained a favourite subject in his landscape painting.

Before becoming an artist, the young Paul Nash had ambitions to be an architect, and there is a very distinct nave-like quality to his portrayal of these autumnal beeches, with their smooth, columnar trunks. The downs of the title are the North Downs of Buckinghamshire, with the distinctive rounded chalk summit of Ivinghoe Beacon in the distance. Nash painted the scene from a sketch made at the roadside in 1929. While the trees have changed, much the same view can still be had from the National Trust carpark at Ashridge.

JAYA SRI MAHA BODHI
Sri Lanka

A gift that has lasted over two millennia, the sacred Jaya Sri Maha Bodhi tree continues to thrive in the spot it was planted in 288 BCE.

Reputed to be the world's oldest planted tree of known age, this sacred fig (*Ficus religiosa*) in Anuradhapura, Sri Lanka, was grown from a branch of the original Bodhi tree (see page 341) under which Lord Buddha gained enlightenment. The young tree was a gift from Saṅghamittā, who worked with her father, the Indian emperor Ashoka the Great, to bring Buddhism to wider Asia. The tree was planted in 288 BCE by King Devanampiya Tissa of Sri Lanka, and remains there still, aged 2,309 years in 2021. Other younger Bodhi trees exist in special locations across the world and continue to be gifted from time to time.

SACRED TREE OF UPPSALA
Sweden

The Temple of Uppsala with its sacred tree, as depicted by Swedish Christian scholar and writer Olaus Magnus (Olof Månsson), in 1555.

The Swedish town of Uppsala was a religious centre as far back as the 3rd century CE. According to one of the earliest written histories of Northern Europe, the *Gesta Hammaburgensis ecclesiae pontificum* by the medieval scholar Adam of Bremen, it boasted an important temple to the Norse gods, and next to the temple, a sacred tree. The tree was said to be evergreen, leading some historians to conclude it may have been a yew, though Bremen was more mysterious, insisting nobody knew what kind of tree it was. However, he does record, chillingly, that a spring near the tree was used for human sacrifices and that people believed that if the drowned body of the victim was not found, the request being made would be granted. This engraving, which appears in a later account by Olaus Magnus from 1555, shows the temple, the tree, and a human sacrifice looking rather more as though they were enjoying a hot tub.

WATTIEZA FOSSILS – THE FIRST TREES

A fossilized stump from a tree that once formed part of the earliest known forest on Earth.

When quarry workers began blasting rock to build a dam at Gilboa in the Catskill Mountains of New York state in the 1920s, they found what appeared to be fossilized tree stumps. This wasn't particularly unusual, because trees fossilize very readily. What was astonishing was their age – estimated at 385 million years, making them the world's oldest known tree forms. It took a further eight decades before the stumps were linked to other fossils, which revealed their whole structure, including a slender trunk and a crown of ferny foliage. Now known scientifically as *Wattieza*, the Gilboa trees grew to about 8m (over 26ft) tall – and in doing so created an entirely new habitat on Earth – a sheltered, humid, resource-rich space in which all manner of animal life could, and did, evolve.

QUEEN ELIZABETH OAK
England

Queen Elizabeth II plants an oak tree in the grounds of Hatfield House in Hertfordshire to mark her visit in 1995.

It's astonishing how many events of historical significance are said to have taken place under great trees. Oaks and yews feature in more than their share, at least in northern temperate regions, partly because as large, long-lived trees they are natural landmarks, but also because their reputation for strength and resilience lends weight to a story. An ancient oak in the grounds of Hatfield House in Hertfordshire was said to be the tree under which, in 1558, Elizabeth, daughter of Henry VIII and Anne Boleyn, learned of the death of her half-sister Mary and that she had become Queen. The original tree died in the early 20th century, and its dead stump was eventually removed in 1978; in 1985 it was replaced by a new Queen Elizabeth oak, planted by Elizabeth II.

'The best time to plant a tree was 20 years ago.
The next best time is now.'

LIVING STUMPS

Above: Sustained by its connections with surrounding trees, this stump lives on even without leaves and has healed where it was cut.

Left: *Playing the Zither for a Crane*, ink and colour on silk, from the Ming dynasty (1540–1550s).

The felling of a tree is not necessarily the end. Many species are well adapted to natural damage caused by storms or animal activity (beavers and elephants both routinely take down trees) and can regrow from a cut or snapped-off stump. This is the basis of coppicing (see page 259).

In species that cannot regrow and thus can no longer make their own food, it is still possible for the stump to live for several years, using energy stored in its woody tissues. In some cases, life is prolonged even longer by the underground connections the tree made with its neighbours during its lifetime. These connections can be direct, via fused roots, or indirect, via networks of mycorrhizal fungi (see page 272). Through these connections, nearby trees can share water and nutrients with the stump of their fallen comrade, and keep it alive almost indefinitely. Some living stumps are known to have survived hundred of years.

CHURCH YEWS

Yew trees are a familiar feature of Christian churchyards – but in many cases they predate the church itself. Yews have long been regarded as symbols of life, and were often an important feature of sacred sites in Pagan religions. As Christianity spread in the Middle Ages, it was easier and less disruptive for the church to adopt these places, and some of the traditions they carried with them, than it was to start from scratch. The yew-flanked door of St Edward's Church in Stow-on-the-Wold, Gloucestershire, is thought to have inspired J.R.R. Tolkien's description of the Elven Door of Moria in Middle-earth.

Fantastically gnarled yews flanking the door of St Edward's church in Stow-on-the-Wold, Gloucestershire.

SYCAMORE GAP
England

Around 1900 years ago, Hadrian's Wall marked the border between Roman-occupied Britannia and the northern lands where Pictish and Gaelic tribes held sway. The sycamore, on the other hand, is just few hundred years old.

Easily one of the most photogenic trees in Britain, this centuries-old sycamore (*Acer pseudoplatanus*) grows adjacent to the Roman fortification of Hadrian's Wall, close to Crag Lough in Northumberland. Its worldwide fame stems from an appearance in the 1991 movie *Robin Hood: Prince of Thieves*, starring Kevin Costner. Aficionados of movie goofs made much of the fact that in the film, Robin comes ashore on the south coast of England at the White Cliffs of Dover, and manages to make it to Sherwood Forest in the East Midlands by nightfall, despite travelling via this location close to the Scottish border for a brawl with Guy of Gisborne. But this doesn't seem to have done the reputation of this singular tree any harm – it was named Tree of the Year in England in 2016.

HALNAKER HOLLOWAY,
England

Holloways are ancient walkways worn deep into the landscape by the combined action of human and animal feet and rainwater.

Now a peaceful footpath leading from the West Sussex village of Halnaker to an intact but non-functional windmill, this exquisite lane was once a highway – part of the Roman road known as Stane Street, which ran from Chichester to London Bridge. It is a superlative example of a holloway (hollow-way), a path between trees that has sunk into the landscape through gradual attrition of the surface by centuries of footfall and erosion.

STANDING DEAD WOOD

The communities of life that adopt standing deadwood habitats are different to those in fallen dead wood, which can be moist and thus decays faster.

For trees, death is part of life. Under natural circumstances, they often die slowly, little by little, and even healthy individuals begin to develop so-called veteran features, such as rot holes while still in their prime. The heartwood is first to die, and diseased or damaged branches can die long before they fall. In this time the gradually decaying timber becomes useful to a huge array of other life. Fungi and invertebrates are among the most conspicuous saproxylic (deadwood feeding) forms of life, but others take advantage of the cavities that form, for example for nesting holes or roosts.

Right: A 19th-century engraving describes the diversity of tree-like ferns that dominated tropical landscapes in the Carboniferous (coal forming) period.

Far right: The famous jacaranda trees of Grafton in Northern Rivers, New South Wales.

Bottom right: Conspecific forest trees of similar size and age appear to respect one another's space at canopy level.

COAL FORESTS

Coal is a combustible, carbon-based fossiliferous rock, which formed from the preserved remains of plants that dominated large swathes of landmasses that are now Europe, Asia and North America, during the late Carboniferous and Permian periods of geological time, roughly 320–250 millions of years ago. In life, these plants, including early trees such as scale trees, lycopods, horsetails and pteridosperms, formed vast, prehistoric wetland forests. While such forests continued to grow after the Permian, the coal-forming era ended when bacteria and fungi evolved the ability to break down the complex molecules from which woody plant tissues are made, making it much less likely that they would be preserved. These massive forests had a gradual but profound effect on the atmosphere and climate of Earth – sequestering carbon and cooling global temperatures – a process the burning of fossil fuels has reversed in a fraction of that time.

JACARANDA
Jacaranda mimosifolia

This sensationally ornamental native of South America has been widely planted as a street tree in towns and cities across warm temperate to tropical regions of the world. In many communities their blooming is a noteworthy event. In Queensland, Australia, the town of Grafton celebrates with an annual jacaranda festival, but students associate the blossom with the exam season and refer to the associated stress as 'purple panic'.

CROWN SHYNESS

Crown shyness is a biological phenomenon whereby trees of the same species growing close together moderate the growth of branches so that their canopies do not overlap, and thus avoid disadvantaging one another by casting shade over a neighbour's leaves.

'THAT NIGHT, IN MAX'S ROOM, A FOREST GREW...'

An image from the film version of *Where the Wild Things Are* by Maurice Sendak.

Forests are the birthplace of stories, from the *Epic of Gilgamesh* via the collected fairy tales of the Brothers Grimm to Maurice Sendak's magnificent, rumpus-raising *Where the Wild Things Are*. Like Gilgamesh, like Hansel and Gretel, and like little wild Max, we gravitate to forests to let our imaginations run free and, in the words of rebel naturalist and writer Roger Deakin, 'to find ourselves, by first becoming lost.'

BARK

Bark structures, clockwise from top left: oak, birch, sweet chestnut and pine.

Tree bark comprises an outer layer of dead tissue, the rhytidome, and living inner layers that incorporate the tree's vascular system, including the phloem vessels, which transport the sugars created during photosynthesis to all parts of the plant where they are needed to fuel growth and metabolic processes. As well as protecting the tree to some extent, the bark also serves as a substrate for other forms of life – algae, lichens, mosses and epiphytes, which can usually exploit it without damaging the tree.

PYRAMUS AND THISBE

Thisbe discovers the body of her beloved Pyramus under a blood-stained mulberry tree, in the classical tale with clear parallels to Shakespeare's much later *Romeo and Juliette*.

In a story first written down by the Roman poet Ovid, Pyramus and Thisbe are young lovers in the city of Babylon, forbidden to marry by their feuding families. Communicating through a crack in the wall between their two houses, they plan to elope and arrange to meet under a mulberry tree. Thisbe arrives first, to find a lion under the tree. She escapes, but leaves her cloak, which the lion tears and marks with blood from a recent kill. When Pyramus arrives he finds only the torn, stained cloth and the tracks of the lion. Overwhelmed by grief, he kills himself by falling on his sword. Thisbe finds him dead when she returns and duly takes her own life. The blood of the ill-fated pair spatters the fruits of the mulberry, turning them from white (as in the white mulberry, *Morus alba*) to the more familiar red, and the gods, sympathetic to the tragedy, decide to make the change permanent.

HERE WE GO ROUND THE MULBERRY BUSH
Europe

Walter Crane's
Arts and Crafts
envisioning of the
mulberry bush
dance (1877).

Here we go round the mulberry bush,
the mulberry bush,
the mulberry bush.
Here we go round the mulberry bush
On a cold and frosty morning.

This traditional children's song has variations in which the central species
is a bramble and in Scandinavia, a juniper. It was sung while holding hands
and dancing in a circle during the chorus then performing actions to the
lyrics in the verses such as 'This is the way we wash our face/comb our hair/
brush our teeth' – always ending '... on a cold and frosty morning.' The
mulberry version may have begun at the women's prison in Wakefield in
the north of England, where inmates exercised around a mulberry tree that
was planted in the 19th century. The tree died in 2017 and was replaced
with a new specimen grown from a cutting of the old.

NORWAY SPRUCE
Picea abies

The flexible branches and waxy needles of Norway spruce are an adaptation to heavy snow, which is shed before its accumulated weight break the boughs.

A native of Scandinavia, eastern and central Europe, the Norway spruce now has a much larger distribution across Europe and western North America where it is planted as crop for softwood timber and paper pulp, and of course, for Christmas trees. Its seasonal significance appears to be mainly a matter of convenience – in older traditions almost any evergreen was used in winter festivals, but the symmetrical shape and regular branching of this species make it particularly suitable for decorating. To identify Norway spruce in the wild, look for the familiar shape, long cones, bark with papery scales and needles with a diamond cross-section and faint pale speckled lines on one side. Those of the similar Sitka spruce are stiffer, flatter and marked with pale bluish lines on both sides.

TĀNE MAHUTA
New Zealand

The magnificent bole of *Tāne Mahuta* is over 16m (52ft) in circumference with a volume of around 250 cubic metres.

Tāne Mahuta is a Māori name meaning 'God of the Forest', and has been given to a gigantic kauri tree (*Agathis australis*) growing in Waipoua Forest in the warm temperate region of Northland, New Zealand. It is the largest and probably oldest of its kind still standing. When the tree showed signs of water stress during a prolonged drought in 2013, 10,000 litres (over 2,000 gallons) of water was diverted from a stream to ensure its survival. A second enormous kauri in the same forest, *Te Matua Ngahere* ('Father of the Forest') is shorter but more massive in girth. Like all New Zealand kauris, these giants are threatened by a disease known as kauri dieback, caused by a mould organism called *Phytophthora agathidicida*, and measures being enacted to control the spread include the closure of affected forests.

TRAFALGAR SQUARE CHRISTMAS TREE
England

The towering spruce Christmas trees that have stood in London's Trafalgar Square every December since 1942 are an annual gift to the nation from the Norwegian city of Oslo. The tradition began during the Second World War when the Norwegian King Haakon VII was in exile in London having escaped the German invasion of his country in April 1940. On this day in 2021 the lights in London will be switched on, marking the countdown to the Christmas festivities.

The towering Christmas tree in London's Trafalgar Square is an annual fixture and a symbol of friendship between the UK and Norway.

THE BODHI TREE
India

A mural of Buddha at the moment of his enlightenment after 49 days meditation under the Bodhi Tree.

The original Bodhi Tree (Tree of Awakening) was a sacred fig (*Ficus religiosa*) growing in Bodh Gaya in the Indian state of Bihar. In around 500 BCE, the philosopher and spiritual teacher Siddhartha Gautama abandoned six years of extreme self-denial and discipline that had left him emaciated, and entered a 49-day meditation beneath the sacred tree, before achieving the enlightenment that led to him becoming the Buddha. The tree became a shrine, but was attacked on numerous occasions, only to be replaced each time (see page 303). The transformative events that took place on the site are celebrated each year on Bodhi Day, 8th December.

GLADE JUL
(JOYFUL CHRISTMAS)
Viggo Johansen (1891)

The tradition of bringing an evergreen tree or branches indoors at midwinter is a very old one. The indoor Christmas tree in its modern guise – usually a Norway spruce decorated with lights and ornaments – was popularized by German royalty in the early 19th century, and in the UK by Prince Albert in the 1840s. Christmas trees soon became the height of Victorian festive fashion, though Charles Dickens was a little disparaging, referring to them as the 'new German toy'.

THE ELY
LONDON PLANE
England

A vast London plane growing in the garden of the Bishop's Palace in Ely, Cambridgeshire, is thought to have been planted during the tenure of Bishop Gunning, in the 1670s. It is the largest of its kind in Britain, with a girth exceeding 10m (33ft), and was among the first to be planted here.

CRACK WILLOW
Salix fragilis

One of the most familiar trees of riverbanks and wet places, the crack willow is named for its tendency to split or break in strong winds. It can grow quite large, but often leans drastically, usually out across the water. Small twigs and branches have the same fragility and snap off at their bases with a loud, sharp crack. Twigs broken off in this way can sprout roots and grow quickly into new trees. Like most willows, *Salix fragilis* hybridizes readily and botanists disagree on whether or not it is, in fact, a hybrid itself (see also page 167).

MONKEY PUZZLE
Araucaria araucana

A towering monkey puzzle overlooks the snow-capped peak of Lanín. Species of *Araucaria* were present long before the Andes in their present form.

This native of Chile and Argentina has been widely planted as an ornamental tree around the world since the late 18th century, so many specimens have had time to grow to their full impressive height of around 30m (100ft). The trunks of mature trees, with their wrinkled, slightly pinkish-grey bark, often resemble the legs of elephants, or even the dinosaurs with whose reign their long history overlaps. It has been suggested that the height of *Araucaria* trees was a factor driving the evolution of exceptionally long necks in herbivorous sauropods such as *Apatosaurus* and *Diplodocus*. The name 'monkey puzzle' is a reference to the extreme spikiness of the thick leaves, but in fact many animals do climb them, in particular squirrels, which do the tree a service by collecting and burying seeds extracted from their cones. Monkey puzzles are now strictly protected in their native range, where logging has led to them being listed as an endangered species.

BLACK LOCUST
Robinia pseudoacacia

With a small and scattered native range in the eastern USA, this graceful species is also known as false acacia. It has been widely introduced as an ornamental tree around the world, thanks to its large clusters of highly fragranced blossom, and the pleasing effect of its compound leaves that flicker in a breeze and show off their blue-green upper surfaces and pale undersides. Sadly, in many places, enthusiasm for the species has turned to animosity: it is now considered a highly invasive weed in Australia, South Africa and even in parts of the USA outside its native range. Once established, it can be difficult to remove, as it suckers readily, and young trees are covered in long thorns.

An ornamental *Robinia* in a wintry Essex, UK, far from its original home in the eastern United States.

345

THE LOST WORDS: WILLOW
Robert Macfarlane and Jackie Morris (2017)

The Lost Words was described by its creators Robert Macfarlane and Jackie Morris as a spell book, offered to conjure nature-words that have been lost from the language of children. Twenty spells are presented as acrostics, and illustrated in triptychs representing the absence, summoning and restoration of each word. The book became a cultural phenomenon following its publication in 2017, with crowdfunded campaigns springing up around the country to ensure it reached the maximum possible number of children. The book also inspired a whole series of other projects, including musical and theatrical interpretations and nature trails. The 'Willow' spell evokes the resilience and otherness of these riparian wizard-trees.

'O open up your heartwood to us will you, willow,
show your deep within, your rough without,
your water-brushing bough, your shoot, your grain,
your knot?

We will never whisper to you, listeners, nor speak,
nor shout, and even if you learn to utter alder, elder,
poplar, aspen, you will never know a word of willow –
for we are willow and you are not.'

FROM 'WILLOW', *The Lost Words: A Spell Book*,
ROBERT MACFARLANE AND JACKIE MORRIS (2017)

Willow, painted by Jackie Morris, is one of twenty nature names being spoken again by children thanks to *The Lost Words* book.

POHUTUKAWA OR KIWI CHRISTMAS TREE
Metrosideros excelsa

In Māori mythology, the crimson flowers of the *pohutukawa* tree sprang from the blood of the hero Tāwhaki when he fell from the sky. An ancient specimen on the clifftop at Cape Reinga, at the northern tip of North Island, is said to mark the point from which the spirits of the dead depart the world. The striking flowers, which appear in mid-December, have long been used as decoration during feasts and festivals, a tradition that was swiftly adopted in place of the similarly coloured holly by European settlers celebrating Christmas.

Pohutukawa trees bloom on the shore of the Coromandel Peninsula on New Zealand's North Island.

HOLLY
Ilex aquifolium

Redwings are among several bird species that migrate south from sub polar regions to take advantage of temperate berry bearing species such as holly.

Among the most instantly recognizable of the UK's common trees, holly can be identified by its glossy, often very spiny leaves (though look higher up – often the leaves out of reach of browsing cattle and deer are much less prickly). The bark is distinctively pale and smooth, with small, warty pimples, but easy to overlook because the leaves remain on the tree all year round. As an evergreen, holly provides vital year-round cover for wildlife, and its bright, festive-looking berries borne on female trees only, attract birds such as blackbirds, song thrushes, fieldfares and redwings in winter. The wood is hard and very pale, almost ivory in colour, and is often used in fine furniture and marquetry, and for engraving. Holly features in the folklore of many cultures, where it symbolizes life, resilience and fertility and was used as protection against witchcraft.

THE HOLLY AND THE IVY

This popular English folk carol first appeared in print in the early 1800s, but is undoubtedly much older, having previously been handed down via an oral tradition.

'The holly and the ivy,
When they are both full grown,
Of all the trees that are in the wood,
The holly bears the crown.

The rising of the sun
And the running of the deer,
The playing of the merry organ,
Sweet singing in the choir.

The holly bears a blossom,
As white as the lily flower,
And Mary bore sweet Jesus Christ,
To be our sweet Saviour.

The holly bears a berry,
As red as any blood,
And Mary bore sweet Jesus Christ
For to do us sinners good.

The holly bears a prickle,
As sharp as any thorn,
And Mary bore sweet Jesus Christ
On Christmas Day in the morn.

The holly bears a bark,
As bitter as any gall,
And Mary bore sweet Jesus Christ
For to redeem us all.

The holly and the ivy,
When they are both full grown,
Of all the trees that are in the wood,
The holly bears the crown.'

18TH DECEMBER

GIANT SEQUOIA
Natural History Museum, England

If you visit the Natural History Museum in London and climb the stone staircases of the Hintze Hall past the vast skeleton of Hope the blue whale, at the very top you will find another giant – or at least part of one. The giant sequoia (*Sequoiadendron giganteum*) from which this enormous slice is taken was felled in California in 1893. It has been recently restored, so that the rings recording its growth over 1,300 years, from the early Middle Ages to the beginning of the Machine Age can easily be seen.

19TH DECEMBER

SOCOTRA DRAGON BLOOD TREE
Dracaena cinnabari

The remote Persian Gulf island of Socotra boasts an amazingly high proportion of endemic trees – about 37 per cent of its native species are found nowhere else. These include the extraordinary dragon blood trees whose English and scientific names refer to the deep red colouration of their resin. The species name *cinnabari* refers to the resin's value as an alternative to the toxic mineral dye, cinnabar. Dragon blood resin, known locally as *emzoloh*, has been prized for millennia.

THE WHOMPING WILLOW

Above: Hogwarts' fantastically irritable sentinel willow, as envisioned in the 2004 Warner Brothers' movie *Harry Potter and the Prisoner of Azkaban*.

Top left: A vast section of a 1,300-year-old giant sequoia, in which every growth ring can still be counted.

Bottom left: Dragon blood trees dominate the arid slopes of Socotra Island, Yemen.

This magical tree grows in the grounds of Hogwarts School of Witchcraft and Wizardry attended by Harry Potter in the books by J.K. Rowling. The willow is a ferocious being, with clublike branches that swipe at intruders. In *Harry Potter and the Chamber of Secrets*, it reacts furiously to the crash-landing in its branches of a flying car carrying Harry and his friend Ron Weasley. It later transpires that the tree is relatively young, having been planted to disguise the opening of a secret passage leading to from the school to a ramshackle building in the nearby village of Hogsmeade. Known as the Shrieking Shack, the building is used as a hideout by various characters.

YULE LOG
Europe and North America

The winter festivals of northern cultures frequently involve light and fire, and there are many versions of the Yule Log – a large piece of timber brought in, often as a gift, at the winter solstice. The log is ceremonially burned, either continuously or a little bit a day, over the period of festivities. In Europe, especially Britain, and subsequently in North America, tradition dictates that a charred piece should be kept and used to light the next year's log.

THE HOLLY KING
UK

One of a pair of pagan deities locked in everlasting battle for supremacy, the Holly King is the winter counterpart of the Oak King (see page 176), and symbolizes winter and darkness. In neopagan art he is often depicted as an old man wreathed in holly; a Celtic version of this persona may have contributed to the modern image of Santa Claus.

SNOWBOUND

Above: High-
altitude spruce
spend months
a year sheathed
in ice, but
avoid freezing
completely.

Top left: A huge
and well-seasoned
log formed the
centrepiece of
winter festivals
in many north
European cultures.

Bottom left: Holly
Man features
in mid-winter
celebrations.

As a general rule, freezing is not good for plant tissues, but trees growing at extreme latitudes and altitudes have developed impressive cold tolerance. In the case of the spruces and firs of the far north, which keep their evergreen needles right through the winter, adaptation to sub-zero temperatures includes the withdrawal of water from cells that would be damaged by ice, resulting in more concentrated cell sap with a lower freezing temperature. This kind of freeze tolerance also requires the trees to be able to cope with cellular dehydration. A second strategy is to avoid freezing through supercooling, which allows water to remain liquid below freezing temperatures. Supercooling of plant tissues can be achieved through the production of proteins that inhibit ice-crystal growth and by the removal of impurities in water that might serve as ice nucleation sites.

COLLECTING FRANKINCENSE

Blobs and beads of resin seep from a deliberate cut in a frankincense tree. They will be harvested by hand after they have dried hard.

Frankincense is dried resin from trees in the genus *Boswellia*, usually *B. sacra*. These tough little trees thrive in the arid, stony upland landscapes of the Arabian peninsula. The frankincense is harvested by making small cuts in the tree, or by removing patches of bark. The tree responds to the injury by releasing thick, white resin, which sets and dries on contact with air to form small, hard blobs. The sweet, woody scent can be released by burning, or distilled for perfume-making.

THE TWELVE DAYS OF CHRISTMAS

Nature printmaker Robert Gillmor's take on the famous festive partridge.

'On the first day of Christmas, my true love sent to me
A partridge in a pear tree.'

This popular but eccentric carol has been a staple of Christmas festivities in the English-speaking world for centuries. The lyrics were published without music in a book for children in 1780, but versions of the carol had been in circulation well before that. It has been speculated that the pear tree in the first verse is actually a mishearing of the French word for partridge, *perdrix*, and that the original 'first gift' was just the bird. The familiar melody is a traditional folk tune which was arranged and published in 1909 by Frederic Austin.

A yew tree outside St Michael's church in Discoed, Powys, Wales, said to be around 5,000 years old.

COMMON YEW
Taxus baccata

One of the world's most venerated tree species, this dark, mysterious, long-lived but poisonous evergreen conifer is a symbol both of (eternal) life, but also death. With the exception of the pinky-red flesh of the arils, which surround the single-seeded cones, all parts of the plant are extremely poisonous to livestock and humans due to high concentrations of alkaloids in the leaves, wood and seeds. Other compounds isolated from yew are literally lifesaving, having helped in the development of the chemotherapy drug Taxol. Yew is commonly found on sacred sites including Christian churchyards, where it also served to deter local herders from allowing their animals to stray. However, many of these trees are far older than the churches they grow alongside, and it is likely that these sites were deemed sacred on account of their trees well before they were adopted by Christianity. The wood is springy and easy to work, and was the favoured material for making longbows.

Białowieża Forest
Poland and Belarus

The vast tract of lowland forest played a vital role in the survival of the European bison or wisent. This large bull wears a radio-tracking collar as part of an ongoing conservation monitoring effort.

The vast sweep of mainly lowland plains that run from the Pyrenees of southern France north and east to the Ural Mountains was once largely wooded. Only fragments of this primeval forest remain, and the largest and most intact of these is the 1,400 sq. km (540 sq. mile) Białowieża Forest, which straddles the border between Poland and Belarus. The forest is home to a herd of European bison and thousands of vast ancient oaks. It has multiple designations, including a UNESCO World Heritage Site and EU Natural 2000 Special Area of Conservation. Even so, large areas of old growth forest on the Polish side are now being logged, in breach of both designations and of EU law.

WESTERN RED CEDAR
Thuja plicata

Above: Western red cedar tree deemed Canada's 'gnarliest tree'.

Top right: Frost-covered small-leaved lime or linden tree in Haldorf, Germany.

Bottom right: The taiga forests of northern Canada and Eurasia, seen here under the *Aurora borealis* or northern lights, comprise the largest terrestrial biome on Earth.

Another potentially vast conifer hailing from the west coasts of North America, the western red cedar is technically a cypress rather than a true cedar. Its habit of growing very tall and only branching at the top makes it an ideal timber tree, with a straight, even grain and few knots. Its timber is light and strong, and naturally resistant to rot, thanks to fungicidal compounds concentrated in its aromatic heartwood. It has been widely planted in temperate regions around the world.

SMALL-LEAVED LINDEN OR LIME
Tilia cordata

The most common linden in Europe has leaves that are always less than 8cm (3in) long, and often less than 5cm (2in). There are reddish hairs on the undersides of the leaves, but only on the joints between the veins. This, and the smoothness and paleness of the bark, distinguish it from the common and large-leaved species. Lindens are naturally rather slow to spread and so this species is often limited to ancient woodland and regarded as a positive indicator of relatively undisturbed habitat.

TAIGA

The coniferous forests that cover most of Canada, Alaska, northern Scandinavia and Russia between the northern latitudes of 50 and 70 degrees are known as taiga or boreal forest. They comprise mainly spruce, pine, larch and some birch and cover over 11 per cent of the land area of the planet. The trees are able to survive temperatures lower than -60°C (-76°F).

'*Your kind never sees us whole. You miss the half of it, and more. There's always as much belowground as above ... If your mind were only a slightly greener thing, we'd drown you in meaning.*'

FROM *The Overstory*,
RICHARD POWERS (2018)

INDEX

Acknowledgements

Humanity's knowledge of these strong, silent companions is older than we are as a species, and yet we still have so much more to learn. It is almost inevitable when writing a natural history book, that some part of it may be out of date before the pages are printed, and given the astonishing recent advances in our understanding of trees, that will no doubt be the case here too. I owe a debt to an extraordinary collective of named and unnamed naturalists and scientists, foresters and foragers, artists and photographers, poets and writers, storytellers and teachers, leaders and thinkers, conservationists and activists whose imagination, curiosity, wisdom and passion inform and illuminate this book throughout.

Many thanks to Tina Persaud for inviting me to contribute to the beautiful '...A Day' series, and to Kristy Richardson for working so steadfastly under the exceptionally tricky circumstances that have engulfed us all in 2020 and 2021. My love and thanks as always to Roy and Lochy who muddled through lockdown schooling while I shut myself away with this project.

And last but never least, my love and gratitude to the trees, who give me breath.

Picture Credits

Every effort has been made to contact the copyright holders. If you have any information about the images in this collection, please contact the publisher.

@ **Alamy Stock Photo** / A. Astes p352 top; Adam Burton p196-197; adrian hepworth p63; A.F. ARCHIVE p243 top; Alan King engraving p163; Alan Novelli p311; Album p36, p170-171, p330; Album / British Library p228; Alex Ramsay p358; Alex van Hulsenbeek p335; Alwim p281; Andy Collins p120; Angelo D'Amico p273; Anna Ivanova p339 top; Anna Stowe Landscapes UK p144; Antiqua Print Gallery p136 top, p354 top; Antiquarian Images p78; Anup Shah p307; Archive PL p338; Arco Images / Hinze, K p43 bottom; Ariadne Van Zandbergen p15; Arndt Sven-Erik p81; Art Collection 4 p89; Art Heritage p159; Arthur Greenberg p104; Art Media/Heritage Images p135; Artokoloro p95, p180; Art Wolfe / DanitaDelimont p194; Art World p266 top, p266 bottom; Asar Studios p51, p182, p317; Aurelie Marrier d'Unienville p776; BAO p4; Bailey-Cooper Photography p258 bottom; Benard / Andia p169; Bernard van Dierendonck p199; blickwinkel p40, p181 (Katz), p237 (Layer), p267 (McPHOTO/HRM), p283 (R. Bala), p93 (R. Koenig), p294 (R. Linke), p264 (Schulz), p302 (S. Meyers), p175 lower centre (S. Ziese); BLM Collection p56; Bob Gibbons p261, p314, p334; Boelle / Andia p34-35; Botany vision p119; Borislav Marinic p42; Brian McGuire p168; Brownlow Brothers p342 bottom; Cameron Cormack p229; Cavan Images p6; Charles Walker Collection p110; Cheryl-Samantha Owen / naturepl.com p360; Chris Dorney p98, p223; Chris Mattison p128; Christopher Smith p129; Chronicle p52, p97; Clare Gainey p299; Classic Collection p60; classicpaintings p105; ClickAlps p215; Colin Varndell p331 bottom right; Colin Waters p232; craig wactor p331 bottom left; culliganphoto p152; Daniel Rudolf p331 top left; David Chapman p31 bottom; David Foster p191; David Noton p348; David Towers p133; DBI Studio p114; Della Huff p25; Denise Laura Baker p293; Dennis MacDonald p301 bottom; Didier ZYLBERYNG p72; Dmitry Rukhlenko - Travel Photos p37; dpa p313; Eden Breitz p131; Edward Parker p115, p136 bottom; Egmont Strigl p87 bottom; Ellen Isaacs p147; Emanuel Tanjala p77; Emilio Ezeza p291; Emma Varley p255; ES RF Travel p96; Ethan Daniels p258 top; Everett Collection p17 top, p66, p322; Everyday Artistry Photography p178 top; eye35.pix p9; Fabian von Poser p188; Fahroni p192; FCL Photography p244; F. Jack Jackson p22; FL Historical 1B p342 top; FloralImages p100; Florilegius p18, p70, p146 top, p256, p312; Flowerphotos p210; FLPA p349; Frank Blackburn p343; Frank Hecker p331 top right; Frank Sommariva p277; Frederik p123; freeartist p201 top; funkyfood London - Paul Williams p276; gardenpics p301 bottom; Gary K Smith p106; Gary Schultz/Alaska Stock p253; Geff Reis p190; Genevieve Vallee p339 bottom; geogphotos p175 top; George Ostertag p138; George Oze p262; Germán Vogel p121; Giel, O/juniors@wildlife p158; Gisela Rentsch p150 top; Glock p270; Granger, NYC. p11 top, p65; Gunter Marx / TA p26; H-AB p329 bottom; Hamza Khan p195 bottom; H. ARMSTRONG ROBERTS p184; Heather Angel p142 bottom; Henk van den Brink p316; Hervé Lenain p230, p240; Hilary Morgan p134; History and Art Collection p23, p218, p274; Homer Sykes p112-113; Iain Dainty p225; Ian Dagnall p140, p285; IanDagnall Computing p315; Ian Sheppard p295; ian west p268; imageBROKER/BAO p130; Imladris p126; Impress p292; Indiapicture Editorial p265; inga spence p299; Ingolf Pompe 4 p173; Ingo Schulz p27; INTERFOTO / History p271; Irina Mavritsina p252; Jani Riekkinen p362-363; JDworks p54; Jeffrey Murray p109; Jesse Kraft p167; Jochen Schlenker p111; Joe Blossom p282 top; Joel Day p174; John David Photography p176 bottom; John Fairhall/AUSCAPE p235; John Gollop p74; John Nowell p356; John Zada p233; Jon Sparks p214; Josh Harrison p14; K7 Photography p325; keith morris news p41; Keith Pritchard p187; Ken Leslie p249; Kjersti Joergensen p179; Konstantin Kalishko p352 bottom; KPixMining p327; Kristin Piljay p344; Larry Geddis p231 bottom; Leon Werdinger p272; Lesley Pardoe p80 top; LianeM p69; Lizzie Shepherd/Destinations p86; Maciej Krynica p269; Marco Ramerini p200; Marcus Harrison - plants p183; Marcus Siebert p361 top; Margaret Welby p345; Mario Galati p248; Mariusz Black p296-297; Marko Reimann p303 top; mark saunders p7; Martin Beache p185; Martin Siepmann p217, p355; martin meehan p259; Matthijs Wetterauw p282 bottom; McPhoto/Lovell p341; MeijiShowa p219; MEMEME p38; Midnightsoundscape p254; MIXA p311; Moritz Wolf p90-91; Music-Images p333; Nataliia Zhekova p298; Natalya Onishchenko p186 top; Natural History Library p306; Neftali p178 bottom; Nhamza Khan p195 bottom; NorthScape p166; North Wind Picture Archives p177; Objectum p17 bottom; Oleksandr Skochko p83; OliverWright p32; Overland Uncharted p280 top; PAINTING p242, p278-279; Panther Media p161; Patrick Guenette p301 top, p328; Patti McConville p255; Paul Brown p336-337; Paul Edwards p321; Petar Paunchev p25; Pete Oxford p206; Peter Barritt p190; Peter Elvin p62; Peter Ekin-Wood p303 bottom; Peter Horree p79, p84; Peter Jacobson p164; philipus p193; Photo Researchers p320, p332; pjhpix p205; PjrWindows p13; Purepix p94; Quagga Media p107; Rachel Husband p175 bottom; Randy Duchaine p8; Ray Boswell p108; Reinhard Tiburzy p241; Richard Becker p304; Richard Childs Photography p275; Richard Faragher p195 bottom; Richard Wayman p141; Ric Peterson p189; RIEGER Bertrand / hemis.fr p122; riza riza azhari p308-309; RM Floral p50 bottom; Robert Bird p201 bottom; Robert Canis p359; Robert Morris p221; Roger Coulam p118; ROGER NORMAN p221; Roland Pargeter p85; Rolf Nussbaumer p250; roger parkes p137; rsstern p103; Ryland Painter p5; Sabena Jane Blackbird p19; Saint Street Studio p157; SANDRA ROWSE p354 bottom; scott sady/tahoelight.com p286; Seaphotoart p46; Selfwood p117; Shawshots p102; Shim Harno p143; Siegfried Modola p75; SIMON DAWSON p205; Some Wonderful Old Things p145; Stefan Auth p226; Steffen Hauser p284; Stephanie Jackson - Australian landscapes p245 top; Stephen Dalton p149; Stephen Saks Photography p323; Steve Hawkins Photography p176 top; Steven Booth p220; Steve Taylor ARPS p24, p146 bottom, p324; Stewart Mckeown p2-3; Studio Light & Shade p20-21; Sunny Celeste p216; Sunshine p87; Tatyana Aleksieva-Sabeva p82; The Artchives p93; The Book Worm p213; The Granger Collection p27; The History Collection p53, p68, p319; The Picture Art Collection p48; The Print Collector/Heritage Images p67; Thoai Pham p142; Tim Gainey p204; Tim Graham p175 upper centre; Tony Allaker p153; Utterström Photography p257; Val Thoermer p243 top; victor pashkevich p329 top; Volgi archive p165; Walter Rawlings p300; Warner Bros/courtesy Everett Collection p290, p353; Witthaya Khampanant p280 bottom; World History Archive p236; Yakov Oskanov p318; Yorkshire Pics p50 top; Zev Radovan p139; Zip Lexing p202; Zoonar/Petr Jilek p288-289; Zoonar/Stefan Ziese p43 top; Zvonimir Atletić p245 bottom.

@ **Bridgeman Images/** Christie's Images p234.

@ **Getty Images /** Barry Winiker p29; The India Today Group p30; Anne Frank Fonds Basel p58; EVERT ELZINGA p59; Science & Society Picture Library p198; GAMBLIN Yann p340.

@ **Mary Evans Picture Library/** Illustrated London News p12; Florilegius p151; Medici p350-351; ROBERT GILLMOR p357.

@ **Nature Picture Library/** Niall Benvie p31 top; John Abbott p57; Andres M. Dominguez p261; Rod Williams p73; Gerry Ellis / Minden p92; Ingo Arndt / Minden p101; Konrad Wothe / Minden p116; David Tipling / 2020VISION p246-247; Eric Baccega p361 bottom.

The publisher would also like to thank the following contributors: p4, p208-209 © Katie Holton; p10 © Brian Burma; p11 bottom, courtesy of The Oxford Times; p16 Ragesoss. Licensed under the Creative Commons Attribution 2.0 Generic License (https://creativecommons.org/licenses/by/2.0/legalcode); p28, p80, 212 and 263 This work has been identified as being free of known restrictions under copyright law, including all related and neighboring rights; p44, p45 (work by Tania Kovats at the Natural History Museum), p287 © Amy-Jane Beer; p47 © Liz Carlson; p55 © BB / Methuen Publishing Ltd; p64 © Nobuo Yasuda; p67 © Spirit of Oak; p72 © JP Stephen; p86 © Agfa the Frog; p87 top © Apartura / Dreamtime.com; p99 © Carry Akroyd; p124 top, by kind permission of the Provost and Fellows, Kings College; p125 © Manx Wytch; p127 © Andrew Harrington; p132 © Carin Wagner-Brown; p148 © Jo Brown; p155 © Nick Hayes (illustrator) and Robert McFarlane (author); p156 Vassto. Licensed under the Creative Commons Attribution-NonCommercial 3.0 Unported (CC BY-NC 3.0) license (https://creativecommons.org/licenses/by-nc/3.0/legalcode); p162 © Keith Deakin aka TreeHugga; p172© Scotland Off the Beaten Track; p203 © James Brunt; p207 © Ben Andrews; p211 © Arthénon / Laurent Bourcellier; p202 © Macmillan Publishers Ltd, Nature vol 525, T.W. Crowther and H.B. Glick, Yale School of Forestry and Environmental Studies, Yale University. Permission courtesy of Crowther Lab Research; p298 © Neil McCartney; p305 © Gareth Wray Photography; p346-347 © Jackie Morris (illustrator) and Robert McFarlane (author), courtesy of Hamish Hamilton.